FIVE ★ STAR
RECIPES

RDA ENTHUSIAST BRANDS, LLC
MILWAUKEE, WI

PAGE 8

PAGE 72

PAGE 89

PAGE 35

FIVE★STAR RECIPES

EDITORIAL
EDITOR-IN-CHIEF Catherine Cassidy
VICE PRESIDENT, CONTENT OPERATIONS Kerri Balliet
CREATIVE DIRECTOR Howard Greenberg

MANAGING EDITOR/PRINT & DIGITAL BOOKS Mark Hagen
ASSOCIATE CREATIVE DIRECTOR Edwin Robles Jr.

EDITOR Hazel Wheaton
ASSOCIATE EDITOR Molly Jasinski
LAYOUT DESIGNER Courtney Lovetere
EDITORIAL PRODUCTION MANAGER Dena Ahlers
EDITORIAL PRODUCTION COORDINATOR Jill Banks
COPY CHIEF Deb Warlaumont Mulvey
COPY EDITOR Chris McLaughlin
CONTRIBUTING COPY EDITORS Kristin Sutter, Michael Juley
FIELD EDITOR & COMMUNITY MODERATOR Susan Stetzel

CONTENT DIRECTOR Julie Blume Benedict
SENIOR DIGITAL EDITOR Kelsey Mueller
FOOD EDITORS Gina Nistico; James Schend; Peggy Woodward, RDN
RECIPE EDITORS Sue Ryon (lead); Irene Yeh
EDITORIAL SERVICES ADMINISTRATOR Marie Brannon

TEST KITCHEN & FOOD STYLING MANAGER Sarah Thompson
TEST COOKS Nicholas Iverson (lead), Matthew Hass
FOOD STYLISTS Kathryn Conrad (lead), Lauren Knoelke, Shannon Roum
PREP COOKS Bethany Van Jacobson (lead), Melissa Hansen, Aria C. Thornton
CULINARY TEAM ASSISTANT Maria Petrella

PHOTOGRAPHY DIRECTOR Stephanie Marchese
PHOTOGRAPHERS Dan Roberts, Jim Wieland
PHOTOGRAPHER/SET STYLIST Grace Natoli Sheldon
SET STYLISTS Melissa Franco (lead), Stacey Genaw, Dee Dee Jacq
SET STYLIST ASSISTANT Stephanie Chojnacki

BUSINESS ARCHITECT, PUBLISHING TECHNOLOGIES Amanda Harmatys
SOLUTIONS ARCHITECT, PUBLISHING TECHNOLOGIES John Mosey
BUSINESS ANALYST, PUBLISHING TECHNOLOGIES Kate Unger
JUNIOR BUSINESS ANALYST, PUBLISHING TECHNOLOGIES Shannon Stroud

EDITORIAL BUSINESS MANAGER Kristy Martin
RIGHTS & PERMISSIONS ASSOCIATE Samantha Lea Stoeger
EDITORIAL BUSINESS ASSOCIATE Andrea Meiers

EDITOR, *TASTE OF HOME* Emily Betz Tyra
ART DIRECTOR, *TASTE OF HOME* Kristin Bowker

BUSINESS
VICE PRESIDENT, GROUP PUBLISHER Kirsten Marchioli
PUBLISHER, TASTE OF HOME Donna Lindskog
BUSINESS DEVELOPMENT DIRECTOR, TASTE OF HOME LIVE Laurel Osman
PROMOTIONAL PARTNERSHIPS MANAGER, TASTE OF HOME LIVE Jamie Piette Andrzejewski

TRUSTED MEDIA BRANDS, INC.
PRESIDENT & CHIEF EXECUTIVE OFFICER Bonnie Kintzer
CHIEF FINANCIAL OFFICER Dean Durbin
CHIEF MARKETING OFFICER C. Alec Casey
CHIEF REVENUE OFFICER Richard Sutton
CHIEF DIGITAL OFFICER Vince Errico
SENIOR VICE PRESIDENT, GLOBAL HR & COMMUNICATIONS Phyllis E. Gebhardt, SPHR; SHRM-SCP
GENERAL COUNSEL Mark Sirota
VICE PRESIDENT, MAGAZINE MARKETING Christopher Gaydos
VICE PRESIDENT, OPERATIONS Michael Garzone
VICE PRESIDENT, CONSUMER MARKETING PLANNING Jim Woods
VICE PRESIDENT, DIGITAL PRODUCT & TECHNOLOGY Nick Contardo
VICE PRESIDENT, FINANCIAL PLANNING & ANALYSIS William Houston
PUBLISHING DIRECTOR, BOOKS Debra Polansky

COVER PHOTOGRAPHY
PHOTOGRAPHER Grace Natoli Sheldon
FOOD STYLIST Leah Rekau
SET STYLIST Melissa Franco

INTERNATIONAL STANDARD BOOK NUMBER: 978-1-61765-633-0

LIBRARY OF CONGRESS CONTROL NUMBER: 2016948965

COMPONENT NUMBER: 116000223H

PICTURED ON THE FRONT COVER:
Toffee Brownie Trifle, page 93
Three-Bean Salad, page 51
BBQ Bacon Burger, page 37
Sweet Sriracha Wings, page 18

PICTURED ON THE BACK COVER:
Prosciutto & Cheddar Breakfast Biscuits, page 21
Apple & Cheddar Mini Scones, page 86
Cannelloni-Style Lasagna, page 77

"YOU'VE *GOT* TO TRY THIS!"

Let's face it, the best recipes are the ones that come with a personal recommendation. They're the tried-and-true meals that are so good that you just have to spread the word.

Inside *Taste of Home Five Star Recipes,* you'll find 178 dishes that our readers tried, tasted and gave a big thumbs-up. Every page is filled with top-rated recipes, all collected in one handy volume.

We've included **four special icons** throughout this book to make it easy for you to find just what you're looking for, whether it's a make-ahead recipe or a meal you can have on the table with minimum fuss. Check out:

> **FAST FIX** Done in 30 minutes or less
> **5 INGREDIENTS** 5 ingredients max, plus staples like salt, pepper and oil
> **SLOW COOKER** Set it and forget it
> **FREEZE IT** Make it now, eat it later

When preparing for a party, choose an appetizer that fits the bill, from hearty **Grilled Potato Skins (p. 13)** to sophisticated **White Chocolate Brie Cups (p. 8).** If you need a sure-fire dish for a potluck, whip up **Patio Pintos (p. 64), Watermelon *&* Spinach Salad (p. 65)** or any of the amazing desserts inside.

Want to make an everyday dinner that is anything but ordinary? Try **Big John's Chili-Rubbed Ribs (p. 73), Carolina Shrimp *&* Cheddar Grits (p. 70)** or **Fontina Rolled Chicken (p. 79).**

If you're looking for real comfort food, check out the chapter of soups and sandwiches, including new twists on old favorites such as **BLT with Peppered Balsamic Mayo (p. 39)** or new-to-your-family favorites such as **Grandma's Seafood Chowder (p. 47).**

So dive right in—every recipe in this book comes with the personal recommendation of our readers. And don't be surprised when you're the one who's asked to share your recipes!

GET SOCIAL WITH US!

 LIKE US
facebook.com/
tasteofhome

 PIN US
pinterest.com/
taste_of_home

To find a recipe
tasteofhome.com

 FOLLOW US
@tasteofhome

 TWEET US
twitter.com/
tasteofhome

To submit a recipe
tasteofhome.com/submit

To find out about other
Taste of Home products
shoptasteofhome.com

PAGE 103

PAGE 27

★★★★★ READER REVIEWS

Check out what home cooks just like you had to say about the top-rated recipes found inside. Flip through the book to find more of what our readers said!

MUSHROOM TORTELLINI SOUP, PAGE 39

★★★★★ **READER REVIEW**

"Grandkids loved these little nuggets. I love them because they are baked, not fried. They were super dipped in BBQ, marinara or honey mustard sauces. Will make again."

GRAMMA AMY TASTEOFHOME.COM

PECAN-CRUSTED CHICKEN NUGGETS, PAGE 75

★★★★★ **READER REVIEW**

"This was delicious! My husband called it 'restaurant quality'! I used fresh tomatoes, basil, parsley and sage out of the garden! Yum!"

ANAHADDY TASTEOFHOME.COM

GRILLED POTATO SKINS, PAGE 13

★★★★★ **READER REVIEW**

"These are so good, better than any restaurant. I served them as a side with our Father's Day dinner and they were my favorite dish. I used a lasagna-size disposable pan to grill them so that I wouldn't lose all the toppings."

KATLAYDEE3 TASTEOFHOME.COM

★ ★ ★ ★ ★ **READER REVIEW**

"This is my favorite way to serve vine-ripened tomatoes. We also use fresh mozzarella cheese. Yum!"

GRETCHEND TASTEOFHOME.COM

**FRESH HEIRLOOM
TOMATO SALAD,
PAGE 62**

★ ★ ★ ★ ★ **READER REVIEW**

"Absolutely delicious. My 10-year-old grandson ate several helpings and wanted to take some home. Definitely worth the effort. Great for brunch or side dishes!"

COOKINAMA TASTEOFHOME.COM

★ ★ ★ ★ ★ **READER REVIEW**

"My daughter just won the county 4-H bake-off with this recipe. The judges loved how light it was. Perfect for any time of year."

PKFARMER TASTEOFHOME.COM

**LOVELY LEMON
CHEESECAKE,
PAGE 99**

**ORANGE CRANBERRY
BREAD, PAGE 85**

★ ★ ★ ★ ★ **READER REVIEW**

"Best cranberry bread I ever made. Great with butter, ice cream, Cool Whip or cream cheese."

WINGSLADY TASTEOFHOME.COM

APPETIZERS, SNACKS & BEVERAGES

★★★★★

Go ahead and start a get-together on a tasty note! This chapter is stuffed with savory appetizers and sweet sips that will be the talk of the party. Looking for a snack for a day at home? It's here, too!

SAUSAGE BISCUIT BITES

I sometimes bake these delightful little morsels the night before, refrigerate them, then put them in the slow cooker in the morning so my husband can share them with his co-workers. They're gone in a hurry.
—**AUDREY MARLER** KOKOMO, IN

START TO FINISH: 30 MIN.
MAKES: 40 APPETIZERS

- 1 **tube (7½ ounces) refrigerated buttermilk biscuits**
- 1 **tablespoon butter, melted**
- 4½ **teaspoons grated Parmesan cheese**
- 1 **teaspoon dried oregano**
- 1 **package (8 ounces) frozen fully cooked breakfast sausage links, thawed**

1. On a lightly floured surface, roll out each biscuit into a 4-in. circle; brush with butter. Combine Parmesan cheese and oregano; sprinkle over butter. Place a sausage link in the center of each roll; roll up.

2. Cut each widthwise into four pieces; insert a toothpick into each. Place on an ungreased baking sheet. Bake at 375° for 8-10 minutes or until golden brown.

★ ★ ★ ★ ★ **READER REVIEW**

"Made these for a holiday get-together and they went fast. I was asked for the recipe, which I happily shared, several times."

CINDIAK TASTEOFHOME.COM

⑤ INGREDIENTS

APRICOT LEMONADE ICED TEA

Every special occasion deserves a refreshing beverage. My tea has a tangy flavor from lemonade, apricot nectar and mint.
—**KAY CHON** SHERWOOD, AR

PREP: 10 MIN. • **COOK:** 5 MIN. + COOLING
MAKES: 12 SERVINGS (¾ CUP EACH)

- 4 cups water
- 7 individual tea bags
- 1 cup sugar
- 1 can (12 ounces) frozen lemonade concentrate, partially thawed
- 1 cup chilled apricot nectar
- 4 cups cold water
  Ice cubes
  Mint sprigs

1. In a saucepan, bring 4 cups water to a boil; remove from heat. Add tea bags; steep, covered, 5 minutes.
2. Discard tea bags. Stir in sugar until dissolved; cool slightly. Transfer to a pitcher; cool completely.
3. Add the lemonade concentrate and nectar to tea; stir in cold water. Serve over ice with mint.

⑤ INGREDIENTS FAST FIX

WHITE CHOCOLATE BRIE CUPS

Try these unique little tarts as an appetizer before a special meal, or save them for a surprisingly different dessert. They're sweet, creamy and crunchy, and very addictive!
—**ANGELA VITALE** DELAWARE, OH

START TO FINISH: 25 MIN.
MAKES: 15 APPETIZERS

- 1 package (1.9 ounces) frozen miniature phyllo tart shells
- 1½ ounces white baking chocolate, chopped
- 2 ounces Brie cheese, chopped
- ⅓ cup orange marmalade
  Kumquat slices, optional

1. Preheat oven to 350°. Fill each tart shell with chocolate, then cheese. Place on an ungreased baking sheet. Top with the marmalade.
2. Bake 6-8 minutes or until golden brown. Serve warm. If desired, top with kumquat slices.

CUCUMBER FRUIT SALSA

CUCUMBER FRUIT SALSA

We always have way more cucumbers and tomatoes from our garden than we can handle. This recipe is a delightful way to use them up. If making it ahead, stir in the banana and peach pieces right before serving.

—ANNA DAVIS SPRINGFIELD, MO

PREP: 25 MIN. + CHILLING
MAKES: 24 SERVINGS (¼ CUP EACH)

- 1 **large cucumber, finely chopped**
- 2 **medium green peppers, finely chopped**
- 2 **medium tomatoes, finely chopped**
- 1 **small red onion, finely chopped**
- 1 **small navel orange, segmented and chopped**
- 2 **tablespoons lemon juice**
- 1 **tablespoon minced fresh cilantro**
- 1 **tablespoon minced fresh parsley**
- 1 **garlic clove, minced**
- ¼ **teaspoon salt**
- ¼ **teaspoon hot pepper sauce**
- ⅛ **teaspoon pepper**
- 1 **medium peach, peeled and finely chopped**
- 1 **small banana, finely chopped**

In a large bowl, combine the first 12 ingredients. Refrigerate at least 30 minutes to allow the flavors to blend. Just before serving, stir in peach and banana.

APPETIZER PIZZAS

To keep a summer kitchen cool, prepare pizzas on the grill! A variety of quick-prep ingredients lets you create three different flavor sensations. Or let your party guests build their own.

—TASTE OF HOME TEST KITCHEN

PREP: 30 MIN. • **GRILL:** 10 MIN.
MAKES: 9 APPETIZER PIZZAS

- 9 **flour tortillas (6 inches)**
- 3 **tablespoons olive oil**

TRADITIONAL PIZZAS
- ⅓ **cup chopped pepperoni**
- ¾ **cup shredded Colby-Monterey Jack cheese**
- 1 **jar (14 ounces) pizza sauce**

MEDITERRANEAN PIZZAS
- ½ **cup chopped seeded tomato**
- ⅓ **cup sliced ripe olives**
- ¾ **cup crumbled feta cheese**
- ¼ **cup thinly sliced green onions**
- 1 **carton (7 ounces) hummus**

MARGHERITA PIZZAS
- 9 **thin slices tomato**
- 1 **package (8 ounces) small fresh mozzarella cheese balls, sliced**
- 1 **tablespoon minced fresh basil**
- 1 **cup prepared pesto**

Brush one side of each tortilla with oil. Place the oiled side down on grill rack. Grill, uncovered, over medium heat for 2-3 minutes or until puffed. Brush tortillas with oil; turn and top with pizza toppings.

FOR TRADITIONAL PIZZAS *Top three grilled tortillas with pepperoni and cheese. Cover and grill for 2-3 minutes or until cheese is melted. Cut into wedges; serve with pizza sauce.*

FOR MEDITERRANEAN PIZZAS *Top three grilled tortillas with tomato, olives, feta cheese and onions. Cover and grill for 2-3 minutes or until cheese is heated through. Cut into wedges; serve with hummus.*

FOR MARGHERITA PIZZAS *Top three grilled tortillas with tomato slices, mozzarella cheese and basil. Cover and grill for 2-3 minutes or until cheese is melted. Cut into wedges; serve with pesto.*

APPETIZER PIZZAS

MINI MAC & CHEESE BITES

Some younger relatives were coming over for a holiday party, so I wanted something fun for them to eat. I wasn't too surprised when the adults devoured my mini mac and cheese, too!

—**KATE MAINIERO** ELIZAVILLE, NY

PREP: 35 MIN. • **BAKE:** 10 MIN.
MAKES: 3 DOZEN

- 2 cups uncooked elbow macaroni
- 1 cup seasoned bread crumbs, divided
- 2 tablespoons butter
- 2 tablespoons all-purpose flour
- ½ teaspoon onion powder
- ½ teaspoon garlic powder
- ½ teaspoon seasoned salt
- 1¾ cups 2% milk
- 2 cups (8 ounces) shredded sharp cheddar cheese, divided
- 1 cup (4 ounces) shredded Swiss cheese
- ¾ cup biscuit/baking mix
- 2 large eggs, lightly beaten

1. Preheat oven to 425°. Cook macaroni according to package directions; drain.
2. Meanwhile, sprinkle ¼ cup bread crumbs into 36 greased mini-muffin cups. In a large saucepan, melt butter over medium heat. Stir in flour and seasonings until smooth; gradually whisk in milk. Bring to a boil, stirring constantly; cook and stir 1-2 minutes or until thickened. Stir in 1 cup cheddar cheese and Swiss cheese until melted.
3. Remove from the heat; stir in biscuit mix, eggs and ½ cup bread crumbs. Add macaroni; toss to coat. Spoon about 2 tablespoons macaroni mixture into prepared mini-muffin cups; sprinkle with remaining cheddar cheese and bread crumbs.
4. Bake 8-10 minutes or until golden brown. Cool in pans 5 minutes before removing and serving.

SHRIMP CORN CAKES WITH SOY MAYO

Feel free to add hot sauce to the dip that accompanies these savory corn cakes.

—**KATTY CHIONG** HOFFMAN ESTATES, IL

PREP: 30 MIN. • **COOK:** 5 MIN./BATCH
MAKES: 2 DOZEN (⅔ CUP SAUCE)

- ½ cup mayonnaise
- 1 tablespoon reduced-sodium soy sauce
- 1 tablespoon ketchup
- 2 teaspoons Dijon mustard
- ½ teaspoon garlic powder
- ½ teaspoon hot pepper sauce, optional
- ⅛ teaspoon pepper

SHRIMP CORN CAKES
- ½ cup chopped onion (about 1 small)
- 1 tablespoon oil plus additional for frying, divided
- 2 garlic cloves, minced
- ½ pound uncooked peeled and deveined shrimp, finely chopped
- ¾ cup all-purpose flour
- ¼ cup cornmeal
- 1 tablespoon cornstarch
- 1 teaspoon baking powder
- ¼ teaspoon salt
- ¼ teaspoon pepper
- 1 cup cream-style corn
- 1 cup whole kernel corn
- 1 large egg, lightly beaten

1. In a small bowl, combine the first seven ingredients. Cover and chill until serving.
2. In a large skillet, cook and stir onion in 1 tablespoon oil over medium-high heat until tender. Add the garlic; cook 1 minute longer. Add shrimp; cook and stir until shrimp turn pink. Remove from the heat.
3. In a large bowl, mix flour, cornmeal, cornstarch, baking powder, salt and pepper. In a small bowl, mix corn, egg and shrimp mixture; stir into dry ingredients just until moistened.
4. In an electric skillet, heat ¼ in. of oil to 375°. In batches, drop the corn mixture by rounded tablespoonfuls into oil; fry 1½ minutes on each side or until golden brown. Drain on paper towels. Serve with the sauce.

GRILLED PINEAPPLE WITH LIME DIP

Serve this dish as an appetizer or dessert, the choice is yours! If desired, the pineapple wedges can be rolled in flaked coconut before grilling.

—*TASTE OF HOME* TEST KITCHEN

PREP: 20 MIN. + MARINATING
GRILL: 10 MIN.
MAKES: 8 SERVINGS

- 1 fresh pineapple
- ¼ cup packed brown sugar
- 3 tablespoons honey
- 2 tablespoons lime juice

LIME DIP
- 3 ounces cream cheese, softened
- ¼ cup plain yogurt
- 2 tablespoons honey
- 1 tablespoon brown sugar
- 1 tablespoon lime juice
- 1 teaspoon grated lime peel

1. Peel and core the pineapple; cut into eight wedges. Cut each wedge into two spears. In a large resealable plastic bag, combine the brown sugar, honey and lime juice; add pineapple. Seal bag and turn to coat; refrigerate for 1 hour.
2. In a small bowl, beat cream cheese until smooth. Beat in the yogurt, honey, brown sugar, lime juice and peel. Cover and refrigerate until serving.
3. Coat grill rack with cooking spray before starting the grill. Drain and discard marinade. Grill pineapple, covered, over medium heat for 3-4 minutes on each side or until golden brown. Serve with lime dip.

★ ★ ★ ★ ★ **READER REVIEW**
"What a fun, delicious way to serve pineapple! Loved it, and the dip totally made it perfect."
GERMANYCOOK TASTEOFHOME.COM

HOW TO CUT UP A PINEAPPLE

With a chef's knife, remove the crown and the base. Stand the pineapple upright and cut down the length to remove the eyes and rind in strips.

Cut pineapple into quarters; remove the core. Enjoy as a refreshing snack.

GRILLED PINEAPPLE WITH LIME DIP

NUTTY STUFFED MUSHROOMS

NUTTY STUFFED MUSHROOMS

Basil, Parmesan cheese and mushroom blend together well, while buttery pecans give these mushroom treats a surprising crunch. Our children, grandchildren and great-grandchildren always ask for them!
—**MILDRED ELDRED** UNION CITY, MI

START TO FINISH: 30 MIN.
MAKES: 18-20 SERVINGS

- 18 to 20 large fresh mushrooms
- 1 small onion, chopped
- 3 tablespoons butter
- ¼ cup dry bread crumbs
- ¼ cup finely chopped pecans
- 3 tablespoons grated Parmesan cheese
- ¼ teaspoon salt
- ¼ teaspoon dried basil
  Dash cayenne pepper

1. Remove stems from mushrooms; set caps aside. Finely chop stems. In a large skillet, saute chopped mushrooms and onion in butter for 5 minutes or until liquid has evaporated. Remove from the heat; set aside.

2. In a bowl, combine bread crumbs, pecans, Parmesan cheese, salt, basil and cayenne; add mushroom mixture. Stuff firmly into mushroom caps.

3. Place in a greased 15x10x1-in. baking pan. Bake, uncovered, at 400° for 15-18 minutes or until tender. Serve warm.

PEPPERONI STUFFED MUSHROOMS
Prepare the mushroom caps as directed. Omit the pecans, salt, basil and cayenne. Add 1 minced garlic clove to chopped mushrooms and onion when sauteeing. Stir into the mushroom mixture the bread crumbs, Parmesan cheese, 3 ounces finely chopped pepperoni, 1 tablespoon minced parsley and ⅛ teaspoon pepper. Bake at 375° for 15-20 minutes or until tender. Serve warm.

BLUEBERRY FRUIT DIP

My kids dig into this dip. What could be better after a long day at school?
—**RENEE SEVIGNY** WAYLAND, MI

START TO FINISH: 10 MIN.
MAKES: 1 CUP

- 4 ounces cream cheese, softened
- ½ cup confectioners' sugar
- ½ teaspoon ground cinnamon
- ½ teaspoon lemon juice
- ½ cup fresh blueberries
  Assorted fresh fruit, graham crackers and/or cookies

In a small bowl, beat cream cheese, confectioners' sugar, cinnamon and lemon juice until smooth. Fold in blueberries. Serve with fruit, crackers and/or cookies.

FAST FIX ▶
GRILLED POTATO SKINS

The creamy topping on these potato skins is so delicious. They make an excellent summertime treat alongside grilled meat.

—**STEPHANIE MOON** BOISE, ID

START TO FINISH: 30 MIN.
MAKES: 4 SERVINGS

- 2 medium potatoes
- 1½ teaspoons butter, melted
- 2 tablespoons picante sauce
- ¼ cup shredded cheddar cheese
- 1 tablespoon real bacon bits
- ¼ cup chopped tomato
- 2 tablespoons chopped green onion

TOPPING

- 3 tablespoons mayonnaise
- 2 tablespoons sour cream
- 1 tablespoon prepared ranch salad dressing
- 1½ teaspoons real bacon bits
- ¼ teaspoon garlic powder

1. Cut each potato lengthwise into four wedges. Cut away the white portion, leaving ¼ in. on the potato skins. Place skins on a microwave-safe plate.
2. Microwave, uncovered, on high for 8-10 minutes or until tender. Brush butter over shells; top with picante sauce, cheese and bacon bits.
3. Grill the potatoes, skin side down, uncovered, over medium heat for 4-6 minutes or until lightly browned. Cover and grill 2-3 minutes longer or until cheese is melted. Sprinkle with tomato and onion. In a small bowl, combine topping ingredients. Serve with potato skins.

★ ★ ★ ★ ★ **5 STAR TIP**

My family enjoys the flavor of picante sauce but prefers it without the vegetable chunks, so I started processing the sauce in a blender for about 20 seconds.

—**KAREN V.** BILLINGS, MT

VIDALIA ONION
SWISS DIP

FAST FIX ▶
VIDALIA ONION SWISS DIP

I've got one of those sweet, creamy dips you can't resist. Bake it in the oven, or use the slow cooker to make it extra ooey-gooey marvelous.

—**JUDY BATSON** TAMPA, FL

START TO FINISH: 30 MIN.
MAKES: 20 SERVINGS (¼ CUP EACH)

- 3 cups chopped Vidalia or other sweet onion (about 1 large)
- 2 cups (8 ounces) shredded Swiss cheese
- 2 cups mayonnaise
- ¼ cup prepared horseradish
- 1 teaspoon hot pepper sauce
  Fresh coarsely ground pepper, optional
  Assorted crackers or fresh vegetables

1. Preheat oven to 375°. In a large bowl, mix the first five ingredients. Transfer to a deep-dish pie plate.
2. Bake, uncovered, 25-30 minutes or until edges are golden brown and onion is tender. If desired, sprinkle with pepper. Serve warm with crackers or vegetables.

FAST FIX ▶
TOPSY-TURVY SANGRIA

I got this recipe from a friend a few years ago. It's perfect for relaxed get-togethers. It tastes best when you make it the night before and let the flavors steep. You've been warned—it goes down easy!

—**TRACY FIELD** BREMERTON, WA

START TO FINISH: 10 MIN.
MAKES: 10 SERVINGS (¾ CUP EACH)

- 1 bottle (750 milliliters) merlot
- 1 cup sugar
- 1 cup orange liqueur
- ½ to 1 cup brandy
- 3 cups lemon-lime soda, chilled
- 1 cup sliced fresh strawberries
- 1 medium lemon, sliced
- 1 medium orange, sliced
- 1 medium peach, sliced
  Ice cubes

In a pitcher, stir wine, sugar, orange liqueur and brandy until sugar is dissolved. Stir in soda and fruit. Serve over ice.

GRILLED SHRIMP WITH SPICY-SWEET SAUCE

These finger-lickin' shrimp practically fly off the platter at my get-togethers. Play with the amount of Sriracha sauce to get the spice level just the way you like it.

—**SUSAN HARRISON** LAUREL, MD

START TO FINISH: 30 MIN.
MAKES: 15 SERVINGS (⅓ CUP SAUCE)

- 3 tablespoons reduced-fat mayonnaise
- 2 tablespoons sweet chili sauce
- 1 green onion, thinly sliced
- ¾ teaspoon Sriracha Asian hot chili sauce or ½ teaspoon hot pepper sauce
- 45 uncooked large shrimp (about 1½ pounds), peeled and deveined
- ¼ teaspoon salt
- ¼ teaspoon pepper

1. In a small bowl, mix mayonnaise, chili sauce, green onion and Sriracha. Sprinkle shrimp with salt and pepper. Thread three shrimp onto each of 15 metal or soaked wooden skewers.

2. Moisten a paper towel with cooking oil; using long-handled tongs, rub on grill rack to coat lightly. Grill shrimp, covered, over medium heat or broil 4 in. from heat 3-4 minutes on each side or until shrimp turn pink. Serve with sauce.

PEACH SMOOTHIE

Whip up this creamy concoction as a refreshing and nutritious snack. You can use frozen fruit, so you don't have to wait until peaches are in season to enjoy.

—**MARTHA POLASEK** MARKHAM, TX

START TO FINISH: 5 MIN.
MAKES: 2 SERVINGS

- ½ cup peach or apricot nectar
- ½ cup sliced fresh or frozen peaches
- ¼ cup fat-free vanilla yogurt
- 2 ice cubes

In a blender, combine all ingredients. Cover and process until blended. Pour into chilled glasses; serve immediately.

CHICKEN SKEWERS WITH MARMALADE

CHICKEN SKEWERS WITH MARMALADE

My father-in-law loved this chicken dish and said that it reminded him of growing up in southern California. What a great way to bring a dose of summer sunshine to cold winter days!

—**LAUREL DALZELL** MANTECA, CA

PREP: 25 MIN. + MARINATING • **BROIL:** 5 MIN.
MAKES: 8 SERVINGS (1 CUP SAUCE)

- 1 pound boneless skinless chicken breasts
- ¼ cup olive oil
- ¼ cup reduced-sodium soy sauce
- 2 garlic cloves, minced
- ⅛ teaspoon pepper
- SAUCE
- 2 teaspoons butter
- 2 tablespoons chopped seeded jalapeno pepper
- 1 teaspoon minced fresh gingerroot
- ¾ cup orange marmalade
- 1 tablespoon lime juice
- 1 tablespoon thawed orange juice concentrate
- ¼ teaspoon salt

1. Preheat broiler. Pound chicken breasts with a meat mallet to ¼-in. thickness; cut lengthwise into 1-in.-wide strips. In a large resealable plastic bag, combine oil, soy sauce, garlic and pepper. Add chicken; seal bag and turn to coat. Refrigerate 4 hours or overnight.

2. In a small saucepan, heat the butter over medium-high heat. Add jalapeno; cook and stir until tender. Add ginger; cook 1 minute longer. Reduce heat; stir in marmalade, lime juice, orange juice concentrate and salt.

3. Drain the chicken, discarding marinade. Thread the chicken strips, weaving back and forth, onto eight metal or soaked wooden skewers. Place in a greased 15x10x1-in. baking pan. Broil 6 in. from heat 2-4 minutes on each side or until chicken is no longer pink. Serve with sauce.

NOTE *Wear disposable gloves when cutting hot peppers; the oils can burn skin. Avoid touching your face.*

ROASTED RED PEPPER TRIANGLES

Full-flavored meats, cheeses and veggies top a golden crust in this appetizer. I recommend using marinara sauce for dipping.

—**AMY BELL** ARLINGTON, TN

PREP: 35 MIN. • **BAKE:** 50 MIN.
MAKES: 2 DOZEN

- 2 **tubes (8 ounces each) refrigerated crescent rolls**
- 1½ **cups finely diced fully cooked ham**
- 1 **cup (4 ounces) shredded Swiss cheese**
- 1 **package (3 ounces) sliced pepperoni, chopped**
- 8 **slices provolone cheese**
- 1 **jar (12 ounces) roasted sweet red peppers, well drained and cut into strips**
- 4 **large eggs**
- ¼ **cup grated Parmesan cheese**
- 3 **teaspoons Italian salad dressing mix**

1. Unroll one tube of crescent dough into a long rectangle; press onto the bottom and ¾ in. up the sides of a greased 13x9-in. baking dish. Seal seams and perforations. Top with half of the ham; layer with Swiss cheese, pepperoni, provolone cheese and remaining ham. Top with red peppers.

2. In a small bowl, whisk the eggs, Parmesan cheese and salad dressing mix; set aside ¼ cup. Pour remaining egg mixture over peppers.

3. On a lightly floured surface, roll out the remaining crescent dough into a 13x9-in. rectangle; seal seams and perforations. Place over filling; pinch edges to seal.

4. Cover and bake dish at 350° for 30 minutes. Uncover; brush with reserved egg mixture. Bake 20-25 minutes longer or until crust is golden brown. Cool on a wire rack for 5 minutes. Cut into triangles. Serve warm.

CAPPUCCINO PUNCH

(5) INGREDIENTS

CAPPUCCINO PUNCH

When I tried this punch at a friend's wedding shower, I had to have the recipe. Guests will gather around the punch bowl when you ladle out this frothy mocha ice cream drink.

—**ROSE REICH** NAMPA, ID

PREP: 10 MIN. + CHILLING
MAKES: ABOUT 1 GALLON

- ½ **cup sugar**
- ¼ **cup instant coffee granules**
- 1 **cup boiling water**
- 2 **quarts whole milk**
- 1 **quart vanilla ice cream, softened**
- 1 **quart chocolate ice cream, softened**
  Grated chocolate, optional

1. Combine sugar and coffee; stir in boiling water until dissolved. Cover and refrigerate until chilled.

2. Just before serving, pour the coffee mixture into a 1-gal. punch bowl. Stir in milk. Add scoops of ice cream; stir until melted. If desired, sprinkle with grated chocolate.

★★★★★ 5 STAR TIP

To soften ice cream in the refrigerator, transfer the ice cream from the freezer to the refrigerator 20-30 minutes before using. Another option is to let it stand at room temperature for 10-15 minutes.

ROASTED RED PEPPER TRIANGLES

SWISS MUSHROOM LOAF

I usually get lots of recipe requests when I serve this outstanding loaf stuffed with Swiss cheese and mushrooms. It's excellent as an appetizer or served with pasta, chili or spaghetti.

—**HEIDI MELLON** WAUKESHA, WI

PREP: 15 MIN. • **BAKE:** 40 MIN.
MAKES: 10-12 SERVINGS

- 1 unsliced loaf (1 pound) Italian bread
- 1 block (8 ounces) Swiss cheese, cut into cubes
- 1 cup sliced fresh mushrooms
- ¼ cup butter, cubed
- 1 small onion, finely chopped
- 1½ teaspoons poppy seeds
- 2 garlic cloves, minced
- ½ teaspoon seasoned salt
- ½ teaspoon ground mustard
- ½ teaspoon lemon juice

1. Cut bread diagonally into 1-in. slices to within 1 in. of bottom. Repeat cuts in opposite direction. Place cheese cubes and mushrooms in each slit.

2. In a microwave-safe bowl, combine the remaining ingredients; cover and microwave on high for 30-60 seconds or until butter is melted; stir until blended. Spoon over bread.

3. Wrap loaf in foil. Bake at 350° for 40 minutes or until cheese is melted.

★ ★ ★ ★ ★ **READER REVIEW**

"I took this loaf to a party when asked to bring garlic bread. One of the guests remarked that it was the best item at the party. Delicious! I have made it several times."

BROWNSUGAR TASTEOFHOME.COM

MINIATURE SHEPHERD'S PIES

Mini pies, sweet or savory, are ideal party nibbles. I knew the ever-popular shepherd's pie would be perfect scaled down. I've also made the pies with ground lamb and a teaspoon of dried rosemary.

—**SUZANNE BANFIELD** BASKING RIDGE, NJ

PREP: 40 MIN. • **BAKE:** 15 MIN.
MAKES: 4 DOZEN

- ½ pound ground beef
- ⅓ cup finely chopped onion
- ¼ cup finely chopped celery
- 3 tablespoons finely chopped carrot
- 1½ teaspoons all-purpose flour
- 1 teaspoon dried thyme
- ¼ teaspoon salt
- ⅛ teaspoon ground nutmeg
- ⅛ teaspoon pepper
- ⅔ cup beef broth
- ⅓ cup frozen petite peas
- 2 packages (17.3 ounces each) frozen puff pastry, thawed
- 3 cups mashed potatoes

1. Preheat oven to 400°. In a large skillet, cook beef, onion, celery and carrot over medium heat until beef is no longer pink; drain. Stir in flour, thyme, salt, nutmeg and pepper until blended; gradually add broth. Bring to a boil; cook and stir 2 minutes or until sauce is thickened. Stir in the peas; heat through. Set aside.

2. Unfold puff pastry. Using a floured 2¼-in. round cutter, cut 12 circles from each sheet (save the scraps for another use). Press circles onto the bottoms and up the sides of ungreased miniature muffin cups.

3. Fill each with 1½ teaspoons beef mixture; top or pipe with 1 tablespoon mashed potatoes. Bake 13-16 minutes or until heated through and potatoes are lightly browned. Serve warm.

CERVEZA MARGARITAS

One sip of this refreshing drink and you'll picture sand, sea and blue skies that stretch for miles. It's like a vacation in a glass, and you can mix it up in moments.

—**CHRISTINA BREMSON** PARKVILLE, MO

START TO FINISH: 10 MIN.
MAKES: 5 SERVINGS

- Lime slices and kosher salt, optional
- 1 can (12 ounces) lemon-lime soda, chilled
- 1 bottle (12 ounces) beer
- 1 can (12 ounces) frozen limeade concentrate, thawed
- ¾ cup tequila
- Crushed ice

1. If desired, use lime slices to moisten the rims of five margarita or cocktail glasses. Sprinkle salt on a plate; dip rims in salt. Set glasses aside.

2. In a pitcher, combine the soda, beer, limeade concentrate and tequila. Serve in prepared glasses over crushed ice.

GARLIC-CHEESE FLAT BREAD

As a snack or side, this cheesy flat bread will be devoured in less time than it takes to bake. And that's not long at all!

—**SUZANNE ZICK** MAIDEN, NC

START TO FINISH: 25 MIN.
MAKES: 12 SERVINGS

- 1 tube (11 ounces) refrigerated thin pizza crust
- 2 tablespoons butter, melted
- 1 tablespoon minced fresh basil
- 4 garlic cloves, minced
- ¾ cup shredded cheddar cheese
- ½ cup grated Romano cheese
- ¼ cup grated Parmesan cheese

1. Unroll pizza dough into a greased 15x10x1-in. baking pan; flatten dough to 13x9 in. and build up edges slightly.

2. Drizzle with butter. Sprinkle with basil, garlic and cheeses.

3. Bake at 425° for 11-14 minutes or until crisp. Cut into squares; serve warm.

DILLY
VEGGIE
PIZZA

DILLY VEGGIE PIZZA

Here's one of my favorite ways to use up leftover chopped veggies. It's a cinch to prepare and you can change the mixture to match your kids' taste buds. Always popular at special events, it tastes just as good the next day.

—HEATHER AHRENS COLUMBUS, OH

PREP: 20 MIN. • **BAKE:** 10 MIN. + COOLING
MAKES: 15 SERVINGS

- 1 tube (8 ounces) refrigerated crescent rolls
- 1½ cups vegetable dill dip
- 2 medium carrots, chopped
- 1 cup finely chopped fresh broccoli
- 1 cup chopped seeded tomatoes
- 4 green onions, sliced
- 1 can (2¼ ounces) sliced ripe olives, drained

1. Unroll crescent dough into one long rectangle. Press onto bottom of a greased 13x9-in. baking pan; seal seams. Bake at 375° for 10-12 minutes or until golden brown. Cool completely on a wire rack.
2. Spread dip over crust; sprinkle with the carrots, broccoli, tomatoes, onions and olives. Cut into squares. Refrigerate any leftovers.

FAST FIX
CREAMY LEMON MILK SHAKES

Several different recipes inspired the combination of ingredients I use in these shakes. The end result is so refreshing.

—CAROL GILLESPIE CHAMBERSBURG, PA

START TO FINISH: 10 MIN.
MAKES: 4 SERVINGS

- 2 tablespoons crushed lemon drop candies
- 1 teaspoon sugar
- ½ small lemon, cut into six slices, divided
- ½ cup 2% milk
- 2 cups vanilla ice cream
- 2 cups lemon sorbet
- 3 ounces cream cheese, softened
- 2 teaspoons grated lemon peel
- ½ teaspoon vanilla extract

1. In a shallow dish, mix crushed lemon drops and sugar. Using 1 or 2 lemon slices, moisten the rims of four glasses; dip rims into candy mixture.
2. Place the remaining ingredients in a blender; cover and process until smooth. Pour into the prepared glasses; serve immediately with the remaining lemon slices.

SWEET SRIRACHA WINGS

Serve my fiery hot wings on game day or any time friends and family gather. If you don't like a ton of sweetness, add the honey slowly and taste as you go.

—LOGAN HOLSER CLARKSTON, MI

PREP: 20 MIN. + MARINATING
GRILL: 15 MIN.
MAKES: 1 DOZEN

- 12 chicken wings (about 3 pounds)
- 1 tablespoon canola oil
- 2 teaspoons ground coriander
- ½ teaspoon garlic salt
- ¼ teaspoon pepper
SAUCE
- ¼ cup butter, cubed
- ½ cup orange juice
- ⅓ cup Sriracha Asian hot chili sauce
- 3 tablespoons honey
- 2 tablespoons lime juice
- ¼ cup chopped fresh cilantro

1. Place chicken wings in a large bowl. Mix oil, coriander, garlic salt and pepper; add to wings and toss to coat. Refrigerate, covered, 2 hours or overnight.
2. For sauce, in a small saucepan, melt butter. Stir in orange juice, chili sauce, honey and lime juice until blended.
3. Grill wings, covered, over medium heat 15-18 minutes or until juices run clear, turning occasionally; brush with some of the sauce during the last 5 minutes of grilling.
4. Transfer chicken to a large bowl; add remaining sauce and toss to coat. Sprinkle with cilantro.

★ ★ ★ ★ ★ **5 STAR TIP**

To easily trim cilantro from its stems, hold the bunch, then angle the blade of a chef's knife almost parallel with the stems. With short, downward strokes, shave off the leaves where they meet the stems.

LOADED PULLED PORK CUPS

Potato nests are simple to make and surprisingly handy for pulled pork, cheese, sour cream and other toppings. Make, bake and collect the compliments.

—MELISSA SPERKA GREENSBORO, NC

PREP: 40 MIN. • **BAKE:** 25 MIN.
MAKES: 1½ DOZEN

- 1 package (20 ounces) refrigerated shredded hash brown potatoes
- ¾ cup shredded Parmesan cheese
- 2 large egg whites, beaten
- 1 teaspoon garlic salt
- ½ teaspoon onion powder
- ¼ teaspoon pepper
- 1 carton (16 ounces) refrigerated fully cooked barbecued shredded pork
- 1 cup (4 ounces) shredded Colby-Monterey Jack cheese
- ½ cup sour cream
- 5 bacon strips, cooked and crumbled
  Minced chives

1. Preheat oven to 450°. In a large bowl, mix hash browns, Parmesan cheese, egg whites and seasonings until blended. Divide potatoes among 18 well-greased muffin cups; press onto bottoms and up sides to form cups.

2. Bake 22-25 minutes or until edges are dark golden brown. Carefully run a knife around sides of each cup. Cool 5 minutes before removing from pans to a serving platter. Meanwhile, heat pulled pork according to package directions.

3. Sprinkle cheese into cups. Top with pork, sour cream and bacon; sprinkle with chives. Serve warm.

SWEET SRIRACHA WINGS

LOADED PULLED PORK CUPS

BREAKFAST & BRUNCH

★ ★ ★ ★ ★

Whether it's a relaxed morning at home or a big gathering with family and friends, these recipes are the right way to start your day. Wake up to delicious!

PROSCIUTTO & CHEDDAR BREAKFAST BISCUITS

When my family visits, I love to make my nephew Robbie happy by making any breakfast with pork and cheese. I created these biscuits as a twist on the traditional breakfast sandwich.

—KELLY BOE WHITELAND, IN

PREP: 30 MIN. • **BAKE:** 15 MIN.
MAKES: 6 SERVINGS

- 2⅓ cups biscuit/baking mix
- ½ cup 2% milk
- 3 tablespoons butter, melted
- 1 to 2 tablespoons minced fresh chives

EGGS
- 6 large eggs
- 2 tablespoons 2% milk
- ¼ teaspoon salt
- 2 ounces thinly sliced prosciutto or deli ham, cut into strips
- 2 green onions, chopped
- 1 tablespoon butter
- ½ cup shredded cheddar cheese

1. Preheat oven to 425°. In a bowl, combine biscuit mix, milk, melted butter and chives; mix just until moistened.
2. Turn dough onto a lightly floured surface; knead dough gently 8-10 times. Pat or roll to ¾-in. thickness; cut with a floured 2½-in. biscuit cutter. Place 2 in. apart on an ungreased baking sheet. Bake 12-14 minutes or until golden brown.
3. Meanwhile, in a large bowl, whisk eggs, milk and salt. Place a large skillet over medium heat. Add prosciutto and green onions; cook until prosciutto begins to brown, stirring occasionally. Stir in butter until melted. Add egg mixture; cook and stir until eggs are thickened and no liquid egg remains. Stir in cheese; remove from heat.
4. Split warm biscuits in half. Fill with egg mixture.

★ ★ ★ ★ ★ **READER REVIEW**

"My family LOVES these! They really impress and are so simple to make."

RANDCBRUNS TASTEOFHOME.COM

CHORIZO & EGG BREAKFAST RING

HOW TO MAKE A BREAKFAST RING

Carefully pull the points of the crescent dough triangles straight over the filling to the inside of the ring. Tuck the points under the base, and bake away.

CORNMEAL-WHEAT HOTCAKES

Drizzled with a touch of honey butter, these tasty hotcakes will brighten the day for everyone at the breakfast table. We sometimes add fruit on the side.

—ELISABETH LARSEN PLEASANT GROVE, UT

PREP: 15 MIN. • **COOK:** 5 MIN./BATCH
MAKES: 12 PANCAKES (½ CUP HONEY BUTTER)

- ¾ **cup all-purpose flour**
- ½ **cup whole wheat flour**
- ¼ **cup cornmeal**
- 2 **teaspoons sugar**
- 1 **teaspoon salt**
- 1 **teaspoon baking powder**
- ¾ **teaspoon baking soda**
- 2 **large eggs**
- 1½ **cups buttermilk**
- ¼ **cup canola oil**

HONEY BUTTER

- ¼ **cup butter, softened**
- ¼ **cup honey**
- 1 **teaspoon ground cinnamon**

1. In a large bowl, combine the first seven ingredients. Combine the eggs, buttermilk and oil; add to dry ingredients just until moistened.
2. Pour batter by ¼ cupfuls onto a greased hot griddle; turn when bubbles form on top. Cook until the second side is golden brown.
3. In a small bowl, combine the butter, honey and cinnamon. Serve honey butter with the pancakes.

CHORIZO & EGG BREAKFAST RING

People go crazy when I bring this loaded crescent ring to parties. I can bake it at home and take it along. Of course, everyone's happy when we have it for dinner, too!

—FRANCES BLACKWELDER
GRAND JUNCTION, CO

PREP: 25 MIN. • **BAKE:** 15 MIN.
MAKES: 8 SERVINGS

- 2 **tubes (8 ounces each) refrigerated crescent rolls**
- ½ **pound uncooked chorizo, casings removed, or bulk spicy pork sausage**
- 8 **large eggs**
- ¼ **teaspoon salt**
- ¼ **teaspoon pepper**
- 1 **tablespoon butter**
- 1 **cup (4 ounces) shredded pepper jack cheese**
- 1 **cup salsa**

1. Preheat oven to 375°. Unroll crescent dough and separate into triangles. On an ungreased 12-in. pizza pan, arrange the triangles in a ring with points toward the outside and wide ends overlapping. Press overlapping dough to seal.
2. In a large skillet, cook chorizo over medium heat 6-8 minutes or until cooked through, breaking into crumbles. Remove with a slotted spoon; drain on paper towels. Discard drippings, wiping skillet clean.
3. In a small bowl, whisk eggs, salt and pepper until blended. In the same skillet, heat butter over medium heat. Pour in egg mixture; cook and stir until eggs are thickened and no liquid egg remains.
4. Spoon egg mixture, chorizo and cheese across wide end of triangles. Fold pointed end of triangles over filling, tucking points under to form a ring (filling will be visible).
5. Bake 15-20 minutes or until golden brown. Serve with salsa.

ASPARAGUS CREAM
CHEESE OMELET

FAST FIX ▶
ASPARAGUS CREAM CHEESE OMELET

When asparagus is in season, it makes an appearance at almost all of my meals. It tastes fantastic in this omelet, and it looks pretty great, too.

—JANE CAIN JUNCTION CITY, OH

START TO FINISH: 20 MIN.
MAKES: 2 SERVINGS

- 4 **fresh asparagus spears, trimmed and cut into 1-inch pieces**
- 4 **large eggs**
- ¼ **cup sour cream**
- 2 **teaspoons dried minced onion**
- ¼ **teaspoon salt**
- ¼ **teaspoon crushed red pepper flakes**
- 2 **teaspoons butter**
- 2 **ounces cream cheese, cubed and softened**

1. Fill a small saucepan three-fourths full with water; bring to a boil. Add asparagus; cook, uncovered, 2-4 minutes or until crisp-tender. Remove and immediately drop into ice water. Drain and pat dry.

2. In a small bowl, whisk eggs, sour cream, onion, salt and pepper flakes. In a large nonstick skillet, heat butter over medium-high heat. Pour in egg mixture. Mixture should set immediately at edge. As eggs set, push cooked portions toward the center, letting uncooked eggs flow underneath.

3. When eggs are thickened and no liquid egg remains, top one side with cream cheese and asparagus. Fold omelet in half. Reduce heat to low; let stand, covered, 1-2 minutes or until cream cheese is melted. Cut omelet in half before serving.

FAST FIX ▶
VERY VEGGIE FRITTATA

We enjoy this colorful frittata often. The sour cream gives the egg wedges great flavor.

—TERI CONDON BURLEY, ID

START TO FINISH: 25 MIN.
MAKES: 4 SERVINGS

- 5 **large eggs**
- ¼ **cup sour cream**
- ¼ **teaspoon salt**
- ⅛ **teaspoon pepper**
- 1 **cup (4 ounces) shredded cheddar cheese, divided**
- 2 **green onions, chopped**
- 1 **cup chopped fresh mushrooms**
- ½ **cup each chopped sweet red, yellow and green pepper**
- ¼ **cup chopped onion**
- 1 **tablespoon butter**
  Hot pepper sauce, optional

1. In a large bowl, whisk the eggs, sour cream, salt and pepper. Stir in ¾ cup cheese and green onions; set aside. In a 9-in. ovenproof skillet, saute mushrooms, sweet peppers and onion in butter until tender. Reduce heat; top with the egg mixture. Cover and cook for 4-6 minutes or until nearly set.

2. Uncover skillet; sprinkle with the remaining cheese. Broil 3-4 in. from the heat for 2-3 minutes or until eggs are completely set. Let stand for 5 minutes. Cut into wedges. Serve with pepper sauce, if desired.

VEGGIE SAUSAGE STRATA

VEGGIE SAUSAGE STRATA

As a retired home economics teacher, I've made quite a few recipes through the years. My family approves of this hearty casserole.
—**DOROTHY ERICKSON** BLUE EYE, MO

PREP: 15 MIN. + CHILLING
BAKE: 1 HOUR 20 MIN.
MAKES: 10-12 SERVINGS

- 2 **pounds bulk Italian sausage**
- 2 **medium green peppers, coarsely chopped**
- 1 **medium onion, chopped**
- 8 **large eggs**
- 2 **cups milk**
- 2 **teaspoons salt**
- 2 **teaspoons white pepper**
- 2 **teaspoons ground mustard**
- 12 **slices bread, cut into ½-inch pieces**
- 1 **package (10 ounces) frozen chopped spinach, thawed and squeezed dry**
- 2 **cups (8 ounces) shredded Swiss cheese**
- 2 **cups (8 ounces) shredded cheddar cheese**
- 1 **medium zucchini, cut into ¼-inch slices**

1. In a large skillet, cook the sausage, green peppers and onion over medium heat until meat is no longer pink; drain. Meanwhile, in a large bowl, whisk the eggs, milk, salt, pepper and mustard. Stir in the sausage mixture, bread, spinach, cheeses and zucchini.
2. Transfer the mixture to a greased 13x9-in. baking dish. Cover and refrigerate overnight.
3. Remove dish from the refrigerator 30 minutes before baking. Cover and bake at 350° for 40 minutes. Uncover; bake 40-45 minutes longer or until a knife inserted near the center of dish comes out clean.

★ ★ ★ ★ ★ **5 STAR TIP**
When a recipe calls for frozen spinach, thawed and squeezed dry, I use my salad spinner. It makes it easy to get rid of the excess water without straining my fingers.
—**EDITH L.** LONGWOOD, FL

LOADED TATER TOT BAKE

LOADED TATER TOT BAKE

I keep frozen Tater Tots on hand for meals like this yummy bake. It's a super brunch, breakfast or side dish for kids of all ages.

—**NANCY HEISHMAN** LAS VEGAS, NV

PREP: 15 MIN. • **BAKE:** 35 MIN.
MAKES: 6 SERVINGS

- 1 tablespoon canola oil
- 1 medium onion, finely chopped
- 6 ounces Canadian bacon, cut into ½-inch strips
- 4 cups frozen Tater Tots, thawed
- 6 large eggs, lightly beaten
- ½ cup reduced-fat sour cream
- ½ cup half-and-half cream
- 1 tablespoon dried parsley flakes
- ¾ teaspoon garlic powder
- ½ teaspoon pepper
- 1½ cups (6 ounces) shredded cheddar cheese

1. Preheat oven to 350°. In a large skillet, heat the oil over medium heat. Add onion; cook and stir 2-3 minutes or until tender. Add Canadian bacon; cook 1-2 minutes or until lightly browned, stirring occasionally. Remove from heat.
2. Line bottom of a greased 11x7-in. baking dish with Tater Tots; top with Canadian bacon mixture. In a large bowl, whisk eggs, sour cream, cream and seasonings until blended. Stir in the cheese; pour over top. Bake, uncovered, 35-40 minutes or until golden brown.

COFFEE-GLAZED DOUGHNUTS

The coffee-flavored glaze on these tasty doughnuts makes them a perfect way to start off the morning. This recipe is also great for using up leftover potatoes.

—**PAT SIEBENALER** RANDOM LAKE, WI

PREP: 25 MIN. + RISING
COOK: 5 MIN./BATCH
MAKES: ABOUT 4 DOZEN

- 2 packages (¼ ounce each) active dry yeast
- ¼ cup warm water (110° to 115°)
- 2 cups warm 2% milk (110° to 115°)
- ½ cup butter, softened
- 1 cup hot mashed potatoes (without added milk and butter)
- 3 large eggs
- ½ teaspoon lemon extract, optional
- 1 cup sugar
- 1½ teaspoons salt
- ½ teaspoon ground cinnamon
- 9¼ to 9¾ cups all-purpose flour

COFFEE GLAZE

- 6 to 8 tablespoons cold 2% milk
- 1 tablespoon instant coffee granules
- 2 teaspoons vanilla extract
- ¾ cup butter, softened
- 6 cups confectioners' sugar
- ½ teaspoon ground cinnamon
  Dash salt
  Oil for deep-fat frying

1. In a large bowl, dissolve yeast in warm water. Add milk, butter, potatoes, eggs and, if desired, extract. Add sugar, salt, cinnamon and 3 cups flour. Beat until smooth. Stir in enough remaining flour to form a soft dough. Cover and let rise in a warm place until doubled, about 1 hour.
2. Stir down dough. On a well-floured surface, roll out to ½-in. thickness. Cut with a floured 2½-in. doughnut cutter. Place on greased baking sheets; cover and let rise for 45 minutes.
3. Meanwhile, for the glaze, combine 6 tablespoons milk, coffee and vanilla; stir to dissolve coffee. In a large bowl, beat butter, sugar, cinnamon and salt. Gradually add milk mixture; beat until smooth, adding additional milk to make a dipping consistency.
4. In an electric skillet or deep-fat fryer, heat oil to 375°. Fry doughnuts, a few at a time, about 1½ minutes per side or until golden. Drain on paper towels. Dip tops in glaze while warm.
CINNAMON-SUGAR DOUGHNUTS *Omit glaze. Gently roll warm doughnuts in a mixture of 2 cups sugar and 1 teaspoon ground cinnamon.*
POPPY SEED DOUGHNUTS *Add ¼ cup poppy seeds to dough along with the sugar. Substitute vanilla glaze for coffee glaze. In a saucepan, bring ½ cup sugar, ¼ cup 2% milk and ¼ cup butter to a boil. Cook and stir for 1 minute. Remove from heat; cool completely. Stir in ½ cup confectioners' sugar and ¼ teaspoon each salt and vanilla until smooth. Drizzle over doughnuts.*

ZUCCHINI EGG SKILLET

FAST FIX ▶
ZUCCHINI EGG SKILLET

My neighbor shared more zucchini from his garden than I knew what to do with. He loved this recipe.

—**DARCY KENNEDY** HENDERSONVLLE, NC

START TO FINISH: 30 MIN.
MAKES: 4 SERVINGS

- 2 tablespoons olive oil
- 2 medium red potatoes (about ½ lb.), cut into ¼-inch cubes
- 1 medium onion, chopped
- 2 small zucchini, shredded (about 3 cups)
- 4 frozen fully cooked breakfast sausage links, thawed and cut into ½-inch slices
- ½ cup chopped roasted sweet red peppers
- 6 cherry tomatoes, quartered
- ¼ teaspoon salt
- ⅛ teaspoon pepper
- ½ cup shredded cheddar cheese
- 4 large eggs

1. In a large skillet, heat the oil over medium-high heat. Add potatoes and onion; cook and stir 4-6 minutes or until potatoes are crisp-tender. Stir in zucchini and sausage; cook 4-6 minutes longer or until the vegetables are tender.
2. Gently stir in red peppers, tomatoes, salt and pepper; sprinkle with cheese. With the back of a spoon, make four wells in potato mixture; break an egg into each well. Reduce heat to medium. Cook, covered, 4-6 minutes or until egg whites are completely set and yolks begin to thicken but are not hard.

CRAB-SPINACH
EGG CASSEROLE

¾ cup finely chopped pecans
4 large eggs
2 cups French vanilla ice cream, melted
2 teaspoons ground cinnamon
2 teaspoons vanilla extract

1. In a small bowl, mix brown sugar and butter. Spread onto bottom of a greased 8-in. square baking dish. Layer with pear, raisins, bread cubes and pecans.
2. In a large bowl, whisk eggs, ice cream, cinnamon and vanilla until blended; pour over top. Refrigerate, covered, several hours or overnight.
3. Preheat oven to 350°. Remove the casserole from refrigerator while oven heats. Bake, uncovered, 40-45 minutes or until golden brown and a knife inserted near the center comes out clean. Let stand 5-10 minutes before serving.

FAST FIX

SAUSAGE BREAKFAST BURRITOS

These are a fun and filling way to serve scrambled eggs, and the zippy flavor will wake up your taste buds.
—**BRENDA SPANN** GRANGER, IN

START TO FINISH: 20 MIN.
MAKES: 8 SERVINGS

1 pound bulk pork sausage
1 small onion, chopped
½ green pepper, chopped
1 can (4 ounces) mushroom stems and pieces, drained
1 tablespoon butter
6 large eggs, beaten
8 flour tortillas (8 inches), warmed
1 cup (4 ounces) shredded cheddar cheese
   Salsa, optional

1. In a large skillet, brown sausage. Drain, reserving 2 tablespoons drippings. Saute the onion, green pepper and mushrooms in drippings until tender.
2. In another skillet, melt butter over medium-high heat. Add eggs; cook and stir until set.
3. Divide the sausage mixture among tortillas; top with eggs and cheese. Fold bottom of tortilla over filling and roll up. Serve with salsa if desired.

CRAB-SPINACH EGG CASSEROLE

I've developed a strong interest in cooking over the years. I came up with this casserole as a special breakfast for our daughter when she was home for a visit.
—**STEVE HEATON** DELTONA, FL

PREP: 10 MIN. • **BAKE:** 30 MIN. + STANDING
MAKES: 12-16 SERVINGS

8 large eggs
2 cups half-and-half cream
2 cans (6 ounces each) crabmeat, drained
1 package (10 ounces) frozen chopped spinach, thawed and squeezed dry
1 cup dry bread crumbs
1 cup (4 ounces) shredded Swiss cheese
½ teaspoon salt
¼ teaspoon pepper
¼ teaspoon ground nutmeg
2 celery ribs, chopped
½ cup chopped onion
½ cup chopped sweet red pepper
3 medium fresh mushrooms, chopped
2 tablespoons butter

1. In a large bowl, beat eggs and cream. Stir in the crab, spinach, bread crumbs, cheese, salt, pepper and nutmeg; set aside. In a skillet, saute the celery, onion, red pepper and mushrooms in butter until tender. Add to the spinach mixture.
2. Transfer to a greased shallow 2½-qt. baking dish. Bake, uncovered, at 375° for 30-35 minutes or until a thermometer reads 160°. Let stand for 10 minutes before serving.

PEAR-STUFFED FRENCH VANILLA TOAST

My handyman, who is originally from Nicaragua, shared this classic breakfast dish his mother use to prepare. He says he makes it frequently for his children and they clean their plates!
—**GAIL BORCZYK** BOCA RATON, FL

PREP: 20 MIN. + CHILLING • **BAKE:** 40 MIN.
MAKES: 6 SERVINGS

1 cup packed brown sugar
½ cup butter, melted
1 large pear, peeled and sliced (about 1½ cups)
¾ cup raisins
4 cups cubed day-old French bread (1½ inch pieces)

SPICY HASH BROWN WAFFLES WITH FRIED EGGS

Refrigerated hash brown potatoes help you make quick work of these crunchy waffles. Put out lots of toppings so everyone can design his or her own.

—NANCY JUDD ALPINE, UT

START TO FINISH: 30 MIN.
MAKES: 4 SERVINGS

- 5 **large eggs**
- ½ **teaspoon salt**
- ½ **teaspoon ground cumin**
- ½ **teaspoon pepper**
- ¼ **teaspoon chili powder**
- 1¾ **cups refrigerated shredded hash brown potatoes**
- 1 **small onion, finely chopped**
- ¼ **cup canned chopped green chilies**
- 2 **tablespoons salsa**
- 2 **tablespoons canola oil**
- ½ **cup shredded cheddar-Monterey Jack cheese**
  Optional toppings: salsa, guacamole, sour cream and minced fresh cilantro

1. In a large bowl, whisk 1 egg, salt, cumin, pepper and chili powder. Stir in the potatoes, onion, green chilies and salsa. Bake in a preheated waffle iron coated with cooking spray until golden brown and potatoes are tender, about 8-12 minutes.

2. In a large skillet, heat the oil over medium-high heat. Break remaining eggs, one at a time, into pan. Reduce heat to low. Cook to desired doneness, turning after whites are set if desired. Remove from heat. Sprinkle with cheese; cover and let stand 3 minutes or until melted.

3. Serve eggs with waffles and toppings of your choice.

SPICY HASH BROWN WAFFLES WITH FRIED EGGS

ULTIMATE BACON-MAPLE FRENCH TOAST

ULTIMATE BACON-MAPLE FRENCH TOAST

A savory update on baked French toast, this is a make-ahead dish that's excellent for brunch and showers. The combination of maple syrup, bacon and nuts makes it impressive and satisfying.
—**JOHN WHITEHEAD** GREENVILLE, SC

PREP: 30 MIN. + CHILLING
BAKE: 40 MIN. + STANDING
MAKES: 10 SERVINGS

- 8 **large eggs**
- 2 **cups half-and-half cream**
- 1 **cup 2% milk**
- 1 **tablespoon sugar**
- 1 **tablespoon brown sugar**
- 1 **teaspoon vanilla extract**
- ½ **teaspoon ground cinnamon**
- ¼ **teaspoon ground nutmeg**
  Dash salt
  Dash cayenne pepper
- 1 **loaf (1 pound) French bread, cut into 1-inch slices**

TOPPING

- 6 **thick-sliced bacon strips, cooked and crumbled**
- 1 **cup butter, melted**
- 1 **cup packed brown sugar**
- ½ **cup chopped pecans, toasted**
- 2 **tablespoons corn syrup**
- 1 **teaspoon ground cinnamon**
- ½ **teaspoon ground nutmeg**
- ¼ **teaspoon ground cloves**
  Maple syrup

1. Grease a 13x9-in. baking dish; set aside.
2. In a large shallow bowl, whisk the first 10 ingredients. Dip each slice of bread into egg mixture. Arrange slices in prepared dish. Pour remaining egg mixture over top. Cover and refrigerate overnight.
3. Remove from refrigerator 30 minutes before baking. Preheat oven to 350°. In a small bowl, combine the first eight topping ingredients. Spread over top.
4. Bake, uncovered, 40-45 minutes or until a knife inserted near center comes out clean. Let stand 10 minutes before serving. Drizzle with syrup.

HAM 'N' EGG CASSEROLE

HAM 'N' EGG CASSEROLE

I like to prepare this breakfast bake when I have ham leftovers and day-old bread on hand. I love that it's prepared the night before, which allows me to focus on making other dishes for brunch.

—**ELIZABETH HESSE** SPRINGVILLE, NY

PREP: 15 MIN. + CHILLING • **BAKE:** 45 MIN.
MAKES: 10-12 SERVINGS

- ½ **cup chopped green pepper**
- ½ **cup butter, cubed**
- 10 **slices white bread, cubed**
- 2 **cups cubed fully cooked ham**
- ½ **pound process American cheese, cubed**
- 6 **large eggs**
- 2 **cups milk**
- 1 **teaspoon ground mustard**

1. In a large skillet, saute the green pepper in butter until tender. Remove green pepper, reserving drippings. Combine the green pepper, bread and ham; place in an ungreased 13x9-in. baking dish.

2. Add cheese to drippings; cook and stir over low heat until cheese melts. Pour over bread mixture. Whisk the eggs, milk and mustard; pour over cheese. Cover and refrigerate overnight.

3. Remove from refrigerator 30 minutes before baking. Bake, uncovered, at 350° for 45-55 minutes or until a knife inserted near the center comes out clean. Let rest for 5 minutes before serving.

GRANDMOTHER'S TOAD IN A HOLE

I have fond memories of my grandmother's Yorkshire pudding wrapped around sausages, a puffy dish my kids called "The Boat." Slather the servings with butter and maple syrup.

—**SUSAN KIEBOAM** STREETSBORO, OH

PREP: 10 MIN. + STANDING • **BAKE:** 25 MIN.
MAKES: 6 SERVINGS

- 3 **large eggs**
- 1 **cup 2% milk**
- ½ **teaspoon salt**
- 1 **cup all-purpose flour**
- 1 **package (12 ounces) uncooked maple breakfast sausage links**
- 3 **tablespoons olive oil**
  Butter and maple syrup, optional

1. Preheat oven to 400°. In a small bowl, whisk eggs, milk and salt. Whisk flour into egg mixture until blended. Let stand 30 minutes. Meanwhile, cook sausage according to the package directions; cut each sausage into three pieces.

2. Place the oil in a 12-in. nonstick ovenproof skillet. Place in the oven 3-4 minutes or until hot. Stir batter and pour into prepared skillet; top with sausage. Bake 20-25 minutes or until golden brown and puffed. Remove from skillet; cut into wedges. If desired, serve with butter and syrup.

★ ★ ★ ★ ★ **READER REVIEW**

"It's time to make this one again! Hubby and I really enjoyed this upscaled breakfast. I used a ground sausage versus the links. I did not serve it with any gravy or syrup, and it was wonderful as is."

APPY_GIRL TASTEOFHOME.COM

GRANDMOTHER'S TOAD IN A HOLE

BRUNCH-STYLE PORTOBELLO MUSHROOMS

I've always loved portobellos for their stuffability. I combined my favorite ingredients for this rich, savory main dish that's wonderful for breakfast, brunch or even dinner.

—**SYLVIA WALDSMITH** ROCKTON, IL

START TO FINISH: 30 MIN.
MAKES: 4 SERVINGS

- 4 **large portobello mushrooms, stems removed**
- 2 **packages (10 ounces each) frozen creamed spinach, thawed**
- 4 **large eggs**
- ¼ **cup shredded Gouda cheese**
- ½ **cup crumbled cooked bacon**
  Salt and pepper, optional

1. Place mushrooms, stem side up, in an ungreased 15x10x1-in. baking pan. Spoon spinach onto mushrooms, building up the sides. Carefully crack an egg into the center of each mushroom; sprinkle with cheese and bacon.
2. Bake at 375° for 18-20 minutes or until eggs are set. Sprinkle with salt and pepper if desired.

★ ★ ★ ★ ★ **READER REVIEW**

"These are delicious. Instead of using frozen creamed spinach, I saute fresh spinach with some scallions, salt, pepper and nutmeg."

LNVERTEBRATE TASTEOFHOME.COM

APPLE-PEAR PUFF PANCAKE

APPLE-PEAR PUFF PANCAKE

Whenever I serve this fruity pancake, people think I worked on it for hours. They're surprised that such a beautiful dish can be done in 30 minutes!

—**CAROL WILLIAMS** ST. JOSEPH, MO

START TO FINISH: 30 MIN.
MAKES: 6 SERVINGS

- 3 **tablespoons butter**
- 4 **large eggs**
- 1 **cup 2% milk**
- 1 **cup all-purpose flour**
- 1 **tablespoon sugar**
- ⅛ **teaspoon ground nutmeg**

TOPPING

- 3 **tablespoons butter**
- 3 **medium apples, sliced**
- 3 **medium pears, sliced**
- 3 **tablespoons sugar**
  Maple syrup, optional

1. Preheat oven to 425°. Place butter in a 10-in. ovenproof skillet; heat in the oven 2-3 minutes or until butter is melted. Tilt pan to coat evenly with butter.
2. Place the eggs, milk, flour, sugar and nutmeg in a blender; cover and process until smooth. Pour into the hot skillet. Bake 17-20 minutes or until puffed and browned.
3. Meanwhile, for the topping, heat the butter in a large skillet over medium heat. Add the apples, pears and sugar; cook 12-15 minutes or until fruit is tender, stirring occasionally.
4. Remove pancake from oven; fill with fruit mixture and serve immediately. If desired, serve with syrup.

CHERRY CHEESE BLINTZES

You can serve these blintzes as an attractive brunch entree or a fun dessert. The bright cherry sauce gives them a pop of freshness. I sometimes substitute other fruits. Some that work really well are raspberries, blueberries and peaches.

—JESSICA VANTREASE ANDERSON, AK

PREP: 30 MIN. + CHILLING • **BAKE:** 10 MIN.
MAKES: 9 SERVINGS

- 1½ cups 2% milk
- 3 large eggs
- 2 tablespoons butter, melted
- ⅔ cup all-purpose flour
- ½ teaspoon salt

FILLING
- 1 cup (8 ounces) 4% cottage cheese
- 3 ounces cream cheese, softened
- ¼ cup sugar
- ½ teaspoon vanilla extract

CHERRY SAUCE
- 1 pound fresh or frozen pitted sweet cherries
- ⅔ cup plus 1 tablespoon water, divided
- ¼ cup sugar
- 1 tablespoon cornstarch

1. In a small bowl, combine the milk, eggs and butter. Combine flour and salt; add to milk mixture and mix well. Cover and refrigerate for 2 hours.

2. Heat a lightly greased 8-in. nonstick skillet; pour 2 tablespoons batter into the center of skillet. Lift and tilt pan to evenly coat bottom. Cook until top appears dry; turn and cook 15-20 seconds longer. Remove to a wire rack. Repeat with remaining batter. When cool, stack crepes with waxed paper or paper towels in between. Wrap in foil; refrigerate.

3. In a blender, process cottage cheese until smooth. Transfer to a small bowl; add the cream cheese and beat until smooth. Beat in sugar and vanilla. Spread about 1 rounded tablespoonful onto each crepe. Fold opposite sides of crepe over filling, forming a little bundle.

4. Place seam side down in a greased 15x10x1-in. baking pan. Bake, uncovered, at 350° for 10 minutes or until blintzes are heated through.

5. Meanwhile, in a large saucepan, bring the cherries, ⅔ cup water and sugar to a boil over medium heat. Reduce heat; cover and simmer for 5 minutes or until heated through. Combine cornstarch and remaining water until smooth; stir into cherry mixture. Bring to a boil; cook and stir for 2 minutes or until thickened. Serve with crepes.

MINI HAM & CHEESE QUICHES

FAST FIX ▸

MINI HAM & CHEESE QUICHES

We bake mini quiches for breakfast with ham and cheddar in muffin pans. Salad croutons take the place of a crust.

—LOIS ENGER COLORADO SPRINGS, CO

START TO FINISH: 30 MIN.
MAKES: 1 DOZEN

- 1 cup salad croutons
- 1 cup (4 ounces) shredded cheddar cheese
- 1 cup chopped fully cooked ham
- 4 large eggs
- 1½ cups 2% milk
- 1½ teaspoons dried parsley flakes
- ½ teaspoon Dijon mustard
- ¼ teaspoon salt
- ⅛ teaspoon onion powder
  Dash pepper

1. Preheat oven to 325°. Divide croutons, cheese and ham among 12 greased muffin cups. In a large bowl, whisk remaining ingredients until blended. Divide egg mixture among prepared muffin cups.

2. Bake 15-20 minutes or until a knife inserted near the center comes out clean. Let stand 5 minutes before removing from pan. Serve warm.

★ ★ ★ ★ ★ 5 STAR TIP

Onion and garlic powders tend to absorb moisture from the air, especially during the summer. Be sure to store them in airtight spice jars to keep them safe from humidity and moisture.

CHERRY CHEESE BLINTZES

PINEAPPLE OATMEAL

FAST FIX

PINEAPPLE OATMEAL

Oatmeal for breakfast is a standard item, but I like to mix it up a bit. This version gets some natural sweetness from pineapple and pineappple juice. It's definitely worth the extra bit of effort!

—**MARIA REGAKIS** SAUGUS, MA

START TO FINISH: 15 MIN.
MAKES: 3 SERVINGS

- 1¼ cups water
- ½ cup unsweetened pineapple juice
- ¼ teaspoon salt
- 1 cup quick-cooking oats
- ¾ cup unsweetened pineapple tidbits
- ½ cup raisins
- 2 tablespoons brown sugar
- ¼ teaspoon ground cinnamon
- ¼ teaspoon vanilla extract
- ¼ cup chopped walnuts
  Fat-free milk, optional

1. In a large saucepan, bring water, pineapple juice and salt to a boil over medium heat. Stir in oats; cook and stir for 1-2 minutes or until thickened.

2. Remove from heat. Stir in pineapple, raisins, brown sugar, cinnamon and vanilla. Cover and let stand for 2-3 minutes. Sprinkle with walnuts. Serve with milk if desired.

BREAKFAST SPUDS

Here's a dish that has it all: sweet potatoes, eggs, ham and cheese. It's a powerful start to the day.
—**ANNIE RUNDLE** MUSKEGO, WI

START TO FINISH: 30 MIN.
MAKES: 6 SERVINGS

- 1 **package (20 ounces) frozen sweet potato puffs**
- 8 **large eggs**
- ⅓ **cup 2% milk**
- ¼ **teaspoon salt**
- ⅛ **teaspoon pepper**
- 1 **cup cubed fully cooked ham**
- 1 **tablespoon butter**
  Shredded cheddar cheese and sliced green onions

1. Bake the potato puffs according to package directions. In a large bowl, whisk eggs, milk, salt and pepper. Stir in ham.
2. In a large nonstick skillet, heat butter over medium heat. Add the egg mixture; cook and stir until the eggs are thickened and no liquid egg remains. Serve with potato puffs; sprinkle with cheese and green onions.

BLUEBERRY FRENCH TOAST COBBLER

I pick fresh blueberries every summer and freeze them with this family favorite in mind. It's a great way to recapture the warmth of past summer days on chilly mornings.
—**MARIE HERR** BEREA, OH

PREP: 20 MIN. + CHILLING • **BAKE:** 30 MIN.
MAKES: 6-8 SERVINGS

- 4 **large eggs**
- ½ **cup milk**
- 1 **teaspoon vanilla extract**
- ¼ **teaspoon baking powder**
- 10 **slices day-old French bread (¾ inch thick)**
- 4½ **cups unsweetened frozen blueberries**
- ½ **cup sugar**
- 2 **tablespoons butter, melted**
- 1 **teaspoon cornstarch**
- 1 **teaspoon ground cinnamon**
- 1 **tablespoon butter, softened**

1. In a large bowl, beat the eggs, milk, vanilla and baking powder until smooth. Pour into a large shallow baking dish. Add bread slices, turning once to coat. Cover and chill for 8 hours or overnight.
2. In a large bowl, combine blueberries, sugar, melted butter, cornstarch and cinnamon. Pour into a greased 13x9-in. baking dish. Cover and chill 8 hours or overnight.
3. Remove both pans from refrigerator 30 minutes before baking. Place the prepared bread on top of blueberry mixture. Spread softened butter on top.
4. Bake, uncovered, at 400° for 30-35 minutes or until toast is golden brown and blueberries are bubbly.

BROILED GRAPEFRUIT

This easy-to-prepare dish lends eye-catching appeal to a winter breakfast or brunch. Brown sugar sweetens the tart fruit, and the sugared grapes add a classy accent.
—**VICKI HOLLOWAY** JOELTON, TN

START TO FINISH: 25 MIN.
MAKES: 10 SERVINGS

- 5 **medium pink grapefruit**
- ¼ **cup packed brown sugar**
- 2 **tablespoons plus ¼ cup sugar, divided**
- 2 **tablespoons butter, melted**
  Seedless red and green grape clusters

1. Cut each grapefruit in half horizontally. With a sharp knife, cut around each section to loosen fruit. Place the grapefruit halves, cut side up, in a 15x10x1-in. baking pan.
2. Combine the brown sugar and 2 tablespoons sugar; sprinkle over grapefruit. Drizzle with the butter. Broil 4 in. from the heat until sugar is bubbly.
3. For the garnish, rinse grape clusters and dip in remaining sugar. Place on grapefruit; serve warm.

SOUPS, SANDWICHES & MORE

★ ★ ★ ★ ★

Juicy burgers, toasty sandwiches and comforting soups, oh my! Turn to this chapter for the perfect lunch or potluck offering. There's something for everyone to enjoy and rave about.

CHIPOTLE PULLED CHICKEN

I love chicken that has a chipotle kick to it. This is a go-to meal when I'm looking for something extra tasty.

—**TAMRA PARKER** MANLIUS, NY

PREP: 15 MIN. • **COOK:** 3 HOURS
MAKES: 12 SERVINGS

- 2 cups ketchup
- 1 small onion, finely chopped
- ¼ cup Worcestershire sauce
- 3 tablespoons reduced-sodium soy sauce
- 2 tablespoons brown sugar
- 2 tablespoons cider vinegar
- 3 garlic cloves, minced
- 1 tablespoon molasses
- 2 teaspoons dried oregano
- 2 teaspoons minced chipotle pepper in adobo sauce plus 1 teaspoon sauce
- 1 teaspoon ground cumin
- 1 teaspoon smoked paprika
- ¼ teaspoon salt
- ¼ teaspoon crushed red pepper flakes
- 2½ pounds boneless skinless chicken breasts
- 12 sesame seed hamburger buns, split and toasted

1. In a 3-qt. slow cooker, combine the first 14 ingredients; add chicken. Cook, covered, on low for 3-4 hours or until chicken is tender (a thermometer should read at least 165°).

2. Remove chicken from slow cooker. Shred with two forks; return to slow cooker. Using tongs, place chicken mixture on bun bottoms. Replace tops.

FREEZE OPTION *Freeze cooled meat mixture and sauce in freezer containers. To use, partially thaw in refrigerator overnight. Heat through in a saucepan, stirring occasionally.*

★ ★ ★ ★ ★ **READER REVIEW**

"Great flavor with plenty of heat. I substituted honey for the molasses."

AUG2295 TASTEOFHOME.COM

SAUSAGE BREAD
SANDWICHES

SLOW-COOKED CHICKEN ENCHILADA SOUP

This soup delivers a big bowl of warm comfort. Toppings like avocado, sour cream and tortilla strips are a must.

—**HEATHER SEWELL** HARRISONVILLE, MO

PREP: 25 MIN. • **COOK:** 6 HOURS
MAKES: 8 SERVINGS (3¾ QUARTS)

- 1 **tablespoon canola oil**
- 2 **Anaheim or poblano peppers, finely chopped**
- 1 **medium onion, chopped**
- 3 **garlic cloves, minced**
- 1 **pound boneless skinless chicken breasts**
- 1 **carton (48 ounces) chicken broth**
- 1 **can (14½ ounces) Mexican diced tomatoes, undrained**
- 1 **can (10 ounces) enchilada sauce**
- 2 **tablespoons tomato paste**
- 1 **tablespoon chili powder**
- 2 **teaspoons ground cumin**
- ½ **teaspoon pepper**
- ½ **to 1 teaspoon chipotle hot pepper sauce, optional**
- ⅓ **cup minced fresh cilantro**
  Optional toppings: shredded cheddar cheese, cubed avocado, sour cream and crispy tortilla strips

1. In a large skillet, heat oil over medium heat. Add peppers and onion; cook and stir 6-8 minutes or until tender. Add garlic; cook 1 minute longer. Transfer pepper mixture and chicken to a 5- or 6-qt. slow cooker. Stir in the broth, tomatoes, enchilada sauce, tomato paste, seasonings and, if desired, pepper sauce. Cook, covered, on low 6-8 hours or until chicken is tender (a thermometer should read at least 165°).
2. Remove chicken from slow cooker. Shred with two forks; return to slow cooker. Stir in cilantro. Serve with toppings as desired.
FREEZE OPTION *Freeze cooled soup in freezer containers. To use, partially thaw in refrigerator overnight. Heat through in a saucepan, stirring occasionally and adding a little water if necessary.*

SAUSAGE BREAD SANDWICHES

I make these sandwiches in my spare time and freeze them so they're ready when needed—especially for tailgating at Kansas State football games.

—**DONNA ROBERTS** MANHATTAN, KS

PREP: 30 MIN. • **BAKE:** 20 MIN.
MAKES: 4 SANDWICH LOAVES
(3 PIECES EACH)

- 1 **package (16 ounces) hot roll mix**
- 2 **pounds reduced-fat bulk pork sausage**
- 2 **tablespoons dried parsley flakes**
- 2 **teaspoons garlic powder**
- 1 **teaspoon onion powder**
- ½ **teaspoon dried oregano**
- 2 **cups (8 ounces) shredded part-skim mozzarella cheese**
- ½ **cup grated Parmesan cheese**
- 1 **large egg**
- 1 **tablespoon water**

1. Preheat oven to 350°. Prepare roll mix dough according to package directions.
2. Meanwhile, in a large skillet, cook sausage over medium heat 8-10 minutes or until no longer pink, breaking into crumbles; drain. Stir in seasonings.
3. Divide dough into four portions. On a lightly floured surface, roll each portion into a 14x8-in. rectangle. Top each with 1¼ cups sausage mixture to within 1 inch of edges; sprinkle with ½ cup mozzarella cheese and 2 tablespoons Parmesan cheese. Roll up jelly-roll style, starting with a long side; pinch the seams and ends to seal.
4. Transfer to greased baking sheets, seam side down. In a small bowl, whisk egg with water; brush over loaves. Bake 20-25 minutes or until golden brown and heated through. Cool 5 minutes before slicing loaves.
FREEZE OPTION *Cool cooked sandwiches 1 hour on wire racks. Cut each sandwich into thirds; wrap each securely in foil. Freeze until serving. To reheat the sandwiches in the oven, place wrapped frozen sandwiches on a baking sheet. Heat in a preheated 375° oven for 20-25 minutes or until heated through.*

BBQ BACON BURGER

Every family has a burger of choice, and this is ours. It's stacked tall with bacon and crunchy onion rings.

—**PAULA HOMER** NAMPA, ID

START TO FINISH: 30 MIN.
MAKES: 6 SERVINGS

- 12 **frozen onion rings**
- 2 **pounds ground beef**
- ¼ **teaspoon garlic salt**
- ¼ **teaspoon pepper**
- 6 **slices pepper jack cheese**
- 6 **hamburger buns, split and toasted**
- 1 **cup barbecue sauce**
- 6 **cooked bacon strips**
  Optional toppings: lettuce leaves, sliced tomato and dill pickles

1. Bake onion rings according to package directions. Meanwhile, in a large bowl, combine beef, garlic salt and pepper; mix lightly but thoroughly. Shape into six ¾-in.-thick patties.

2. In a large nonstick skillet, cook burgers over medium heat 5-7 minutes on each side or until a thermometer reads 160°, adding cheese during the last minute of cooking. Serve on buns with barbecue sauce, bacon, onion rings and toppings as desired.

HOW TO TEST BURGER DONENESS

Wondering if your burger is cooked to perfection? To test for doneness, hold the burger with tongs and insert an instant-read thermometer horizontally from the side. Insert the thermometer far enough to measure the temperature in the center.

Beef, pork and lamb burgers should be cooked to 160°; cook chicken or turkey burgers to 165°.

SLOW-COOKED CHICKEN ENCHILADA SOUP

BBQ BACON BURGER

AVOCADO QUESADILLAS

AVOCADO QUESADILLAS

Avocados give quesadillas some nutritional value and, fortunately, my son likes them. Slice the avocado thinly. Add chicken or beef for extra protein if you like.

—**DEBBIE LIMAS** NORTH ANDOVER, MA

START TO FINISH: 20 MIN.
MAKES: 4 SERVINGS (2 QUESADILLAS EACH)

- 1 tablespoon canola oil
- 16 corn tortillas (6 inches)
- 2 cups (8 ounces) shredded Mexican cheese blend
- 1 cup pico de gallo
- 1 large ripe avocado, peeled and thinly sliced
- 3 tablespoons minced fresh cilantro
  Additional pico de gallo

1. Grease a griddle with oil; heat over medium heat. Lightly sprinkle tortillas with water to moisten.
2. Place eight tortillas on griddle; sprinkle with cheese. After cheese has melted slightly, top with 1 cup pico de gallo, avocado and cilantro. Top with remaining tortillas.
3. Cook 3-4 minutes on each side or until lightly browned and cheese is melted. Serve with additional pico de gallo.

★ ★ ★ ★ ★ **READER REVIEW**

"This recipe was really delicious and my whole family enjoyed it! I changed it a little bit by using guacamole instead of avocado. I did this because prep time was faster and I could get dinner on the table quickly."

ANGEL182009 TASTEOFHOME.COM

HOW TO SLICE AVOCADOS

- Cut into the ripe avocado from stem to stern until you hit the seed. Repeat to cut the avocado into quarters.
- Twist to separate.
- Pull out the seed.
- Pull the skin back like a banana peel. Slice as you like.

MUSHROOM TORTELLINI SOUP

MUSHROOM TORTELLINI SOUP

This good-for-you veggie soup is filled with satisfying cheese tortellini. It'll warm you up on a cold or rainy day.
—**JEN LUCAS** BALDWINVILLE, MA

START TO FINISH: 25 MIN.
MAKES: 6 SERVINGS

- 2 **tablespoons olive oil**
- ½ **pound sliced fresh mushrooms**
- 2 **garlic cloves, minced**
- 4 **cups vegetable broth**
- 1 **can (14½ ounces) diced tomatoes with basil, oregano and garlic, undrained**
- 1 **package (19 ounces) frozen cheese tortellini**
- 2 **cups fresh baby spinach, coarsely chopped**
- ⅛ **teaspoon pepper**
  Shredded Parmesan cheese, optional

1. In a Dutch oven, heat the oil over medium-high heat. Add mushrooms; cook and stir 6-8 minutes or until tender. Add garlic; cook 1 minute longer.
2. Add broth and tomatoes; bring to a boil. Add the tortellini; cook, uncovered, 3-4 minutes or just until tortellini float (do not boil). Stir in spinach and pepper; cook just until spinach is wilted. If desired, serve with cheese.

BLT WITH PEPPERED BALSAMIC MAYO

Here's my twist on a classic—creamy avocado, balsamic mayo and crisp salad greens make this BLT legendary in my book. For a lighter take, I often use turkey bacon.
—**AMI BOYER** SAN FRANCISCO, CA

START TO FINISH: 25 MIN.
MAKES: 4 SERVINGS

- 8 **bacon strips, halved**
- ½ **cup mayonnaise**
- 1 **tablespoon balsamic vinegar**
- ½ **teaspoon pepper**
- ⅛ **teaspoon salt**
- 8 **slices bread, toasted**
- 2 **cups spring mix salad greens**
- 8 **cherry tomatoes, sliced**
- 1 **medium ripe avocado, peeled and sliced**

1. In a large skillet, cook bacon over medium heat until crisp. Remove to paper towels to drain.
2. In a small bowl, mix mayonnaise, vinegar, pepper and salt. Spread half of the mixture over four toast slices. Layer with bacon, salad greens, tomatoes and avocado. Spread remaining mayonnaise over remaining toast; place over top.

SUPER FAST MEXICAN SOUP

We take this spicy soup to rodeos on cool nights or sip it by a campfire. For toppings, try onions, avocado, cheese, jalapenos, sour cream or salsa.
—**GLORIA HUSE** SIMPSONVILLE, SC

START TO FINISH: 25 MIN.
MAKES: 4 SERVINGS

- 2 **teaspoons olive oil**
- 1 **pound boneless skinless chicken thighs, cut into ¾-inch pieces**
- 1 **tablespoon reduced-sodium taco seasoning**
- 1 **cup frozen corn**
- 1 **cup salsa**
- 1 **carton (32 ounces) reduced-sodium chicken broth**

1. In a large saucepan, heat oil over medium-high heat. Add chicken; cook and stir 6-8 minutes or until no longer pink. Stir in taco seasoning.
2. Add the remaining ingredients; bring to a boil. Reduce the heat; simmer, uncovered, 5 minutes to allow flavors to blend. Skim fat before serving.

BLT WITH PEPPERED BALSAMIC MAYO

BEEF STROGANOFF SANDWICHES

BEEF STROGANOFF SANDWICHES

For an American take on classic Russian comfort food, we turn beef stroganoff into a sandwich. It comes together fast, and our family devours it.

—ALISON GARCIA BEATRICE, NE

START TO FINISH: 25 MIN.
MAKES: 6 SERVINGS

- 1 **pound ground beef**
- 1 **cup sliced fresh mushrooms**
- 1 **small green pepper, finely chopped**
- 1 **small onion, finely chopped**
- 1 **envelope ranch dip mix**
- ¾ **cup sour cream**
- 1 **loaf (about 8 ounces) French bread**
- 2 **cups (8 ounces) shredded part-skim mozzarella cheese**

1. Preheat broiler. In a large skillet, cook beef, mushrooms, pepper and onion over medium-high heat 8-10 minutes or until beef is no longer pink, breaking up beef into crumbles; drain. Stir in dip mix and sour cream.

2. Cut French bread horizontally in half; place halves on a baking sheet, cut side up. Broil 3-4 in. from heat 1-2 minutes or until lightly toasted. Remove from broiler.

3. Spoon the beef mixture over bread. Sprinkle with cheese. Broil 1-2 minutes longer or until cheese is lightly browned. To serve, cut each into three pieces.

SPICE IT UP SOUP

Turkey Italian sausage and jalapeno peppers add kick to this chunky, meaty soup. My husband really enjoys it, so I make plenty and freeze what's left in individual servings for his lunches.

—GUYLA COOPER ENVILLE, TN

PREP: 10 MIN. • **COOK:** 40 MIN.
MAKES: 8 SERVINGS (2½ QUARTS)

- 1 **pound uncooked hot turkey Italian sausage links, sliced**
- ½ **pound lean ground beef (90% lean)**
- 1 **large onion, chopped**
- 1 **medium green pepper, chopped**
- 3 **garlic cloves, minced**
- 2 **cans (14½ ounces each) beef broth**
- 2 **cups water**
- 2 **cups fresh or frozen corn**
- 1 **can (14½ ounces) diced tomatoes with green chilies, undrained**
- 1 **cup diced carrots**
- ⅓ **cup minced fresh cilantro**
- 2 **jalapeno peppers, seeded and chopped**
- ½ **teaspoon salt**
- ½ **teaspoon ground cumin**

1. In a Dutch oven, cook sausage, beef, onion and green pepper over medium heat until meat is no longer pink. Add garlic; cook 1 minute longer. Drain.

2. Stir in the remaining ingredients. Bring to a boil. Reduce heat; cover and simmer for 30-40 minutes to allow flavors to blend.

NOTE *Wear disposable gloves when cutting hot peppers; the oils can burn skin. Avoid touching your face.*

TURKEY CHILI WITH PASTA

We think this hearty chili is the ultimate comfort food. It's a perfect warmer on chilly autumn nights.
—**PAT SCHMELING** GERMANTOWN, WI

PREP: 10 MIN. • **COOK:** 30 MIN.
MAKES: 10 SERVINGS (4 QUARTS)

- 1 **package (20 ounces) lean ground turkey**
- 3 **celery ribs with leaves, chopped**
- 1 **large green pepper, chopped**
- 1 **large onion, chopped**
- 2 **garlic cloves, minced**
- 1 **can (46 ounces) tomato juice**
- 1 **can (11½ ounces) V8 juice**
- 2 **cans (8 ounces each) tomato sauce**
- 2 **tablespoons brown sugar**
- 2 **tablespoons chili powder**
- ½ **teaspoon salt**
- ½ **teaspoon ground cumin**
- ¼ **teaspoon pepper**
- 1 **bay leaf**
- 1 **cup uncooked elbow macaroni**
- 2 **cans (16 ounces each) kidney beans, rinsed and drained**
  Optional toppings: sour cream, shredded cheddar cheese, thinly sliced green onions and ripe olives

1. In a Dutch oven, cook the turkey, celery, green pepper, onion and garlic over medium heat until meat is no longer pink. Add the juices, tomato sauce, brown sugar, seasonings and bay leaf. Bring to a boil. Reduce heat; simmer, uncovered, for 20 minutes.

2. Meanwhile, cook macaroni according to package directions; drain. Add beans and macaroni to turkey mixture; heat through. Discard bay leaf before serving. Garnish the servings with toppings of your choice.

★ ★ ★ ★ ★ **5 STAR TIP**

Wondering why it says to rinse and drain canned beans before including them in a recipe? The answer: salt! Canned beans contain extra salt because of the canning process, so rinsing and draining will cut back on sodium.

CHEDDAR POTATO CHOWDER

CHEDDAR POTATO CHOWDER

I changed up the original recipe to include healthier ingredients, and now we eat this rich, flavorful chowder more often.
—**ELLIE RAUSCH** GOODSOIL, SK

PREP: 20 MIN. • **COOK:** 20 MIN.
MAKES: 7 SERVINGS

- 2 **cups water**
- 2 **cups diced unpeeled red potatoes**
- 1 **cup diced carrot**
- ½ **cup diced celery**
- ¼ **cup chopped onion**
- 1 **teaspoon salt**
- ¼ **teaspoon pepper**
- ¼ **cup all-purpose flour**
- 2 **cups 2% milk**
- 2 **cups (8 ounces) shredded reduced-fat cheddar cheese**
- 1 **cup cubed fully cooked lean ham**

1. In a Dutch oven, combine the first seven ingredients. Bring to a boil. Reduce heat; cover and simmer for 10-12 minutes or until tender.

2. Meanwhile, place flour in a large saucepan; gradually whisk in milk. Bring to a boil over medium heat; cook and stir for 2 minutes or until thickened. Remove from the heat. Add cheese; stir until melted. Stir the ham and the cheese sauce into undrained vegetables; stir until combined.

★ ★ ★ ★ ★ **READER REVIEW**

"I made this for dinner tonight. It was quite good, but I added ½ teaspoon each salt, pepper and Italian seasoning, and 1 teaspoon garlic powder."
JASTICKNEY TASTEOFHOME.COM

ITALIAN SAUSAGE & ZUCCHINI SOUP

Everyone in my family likes this soup. Sometimes I use mini farfalle instead of orzo, because my grandchildren say it looks like tiny butterflies. The recipe also works in a slow cooker.

—NANCY MURPHY MOUNT DORA, FL

START TO FINISH: 30 MIN.
MAKES: 6 SERVINGS

- ½ pound bulk Italian sausage
- 1 medium onion, chopped
- 1 medium green pepper, chopped
- 3 cups beef broth
- 1 can (14½ ounces) diced tomatoes, undrained
- 1 tablespoon minced fresh basil or 1 teaspoon dried basil
- 1 tablespoon minced fresh parsley or 1 teaspoon dried parsley flakes
- 1 medium zucchini, cut into ½-inch pieces
- ½ cup uncooked orzo pasta

1. In a large saucepan, cook sausage, onion and pepper over medium heat 4-6 minutes or until sausage is no longer pink and vegetables are tender, breaking up sausage into crumbles; drain.
2. Add the broth, tomatoes, basil and parsley; bring to a boil. Stir in zucchini and orzo; return to a boil. Cook, covered, 10-12 minutes or until zucchini and orzo are tender.

★ ★ ★ ★ ★ **READER REVIEW**
"Very simple, and using garden fresh veggies and herbs makes it burst with flavor!"
REDHEN1970 TASTEOFHOME.COM

CUBAN-STYLE PORK SANDWICHES

Loaded with tang, this is a lighter version of a favorite restaurant-style sandwich. If you don't have a panini maker, tuck the sandwiches under the broiler until the bread is browned and the cheese melted.

—ROBIN HAAS CRANSTON, RI

PREP: 20 MIN.
COOK: 6 HOURS + STANDING
MAKES: 10 SERVINGS

- 1 large onion, cut into wedges
- ¾ cup reduced-sodium chicken broth
- 1 cup minced fresh parsley
- 7 garlic cloves, minced and divided
- 2 tablespoons cider vinegar
- 1 tablespoon plus 1½ teaspoons lemon juice, divided
- 2 teaspoons ground cumin
- 1 teaspoon ground mustard
- 1 teaspoon dried oregano
- ½ teaspoon salt
- ½ teaspoon pepper
- 1 boneless pork shoulder butt roast (3 to 4 pounds)
- 1¼ cups fat-free mayonnaise
- 2 tablespoons Dijon mustard
- 10 whole wheat hamburger buns, split
- 1¼ cups (5 ounces) shredded reduced-fat Swiss cheese
- 1 medium onion, thinly sliced and separated into rings
- 2 whole dill pickles, sliced

1. Place onion wedges and broth in a 5-qt. slow cooker. In a small bowl, combine the parsley, 5 garlic cloves, vinegar, 1 tablespoon lemon juice, cumin, mustard, oregano, salt and pepper; rub over pork. Add to slow cooker. Cover and cook on low for 6-8 hours or until the meat is tender.
2. Remove the meat; let stand for 10 minutes before slicing. In another small bowl, combine the mayonnaise, Dijon mustard and remaining garlic and lemon juice; spread over buns. Layer bun bottoms with pork, cheese, sliced onion and pickles; replace tops.
3. Cook on a panini maker or indoor grill for 2-3 minutes or until the buns are browned and cheese is melted.

SPINACH & FETA BURGERS

Turkey burgers have their fans, but we prefer burgers of ground beef, spinach and feta. We serve them on toasted buns with lettuce, tomato and tzatziki sauce.

—SUSAN STETZEL GAINESVILLE, NY

PREP: 25 MIN. • **GRILL:** 15 MIN.
MAKES: 8 SERVINGS

- 1 tablespoon olive oil
- 2 shallots, chopped
- 2½ cups fresh baby spinach, coarsely chopped
- 3 garlic cloves, minced
- ⅔ cup crumbled feta cheese
- ¾ teaspoon Greek seasoning
- ½ teaspoon salt
- ¼ teaspoon pepper
- 2 pounds lean ground beef (90% lean)
- 8 whole wheat hamburger buns, split
  Optional toppings: refrigerated tzatziki sauce, fresh baby spinach and tomato slices

1. In a large skillet, heat the oil over medium-high heat. Add shallots; cook and stir 1-2 minutes or until tender. Add spinach and garlic; cook 30-45 seconds longer or until spinach is wilted. Transfer to a large bowl; cool slightly.
2. Stir the feta cheese and seasonings into spinach. Add the beef; mix lightly but thoroughly. Shape into eight ½-in.-thick patties.
3. Grill the burgers, covered, over medium heat 6-8 minutes on each side or until a thermometer reads 160°. Grill buns over medium heat, cut side down, for 30-60 seconds or until toasted. Serve burgers on buns with toppings if desired.
FREEZE OPTION *Place patties on a plastic wrap-lined baking sheet; wrap and freeze until firm. Remove from pan and transfer to a resealable plastic freezer bag; return to freezer. To use, cook the frozen patties as directed, increasing time as necessary for a thermometer to read 160°.*

HOW TO MAKE A TOPPER TIN

Use a muffin tin to double as a handy condiment caddy. Fill each compartment with your favorite toppings, and add mini serving spoons so guests can load up their burgers or hot dogs as they like.

SPINACH & FETA BURGERS

NEBRASKA'S STUFFED BEEF SANDWICHES

When I moved to Nebraska, a friend introduced me to this German-Russian beef sandwich. I'm delighted that my family requests it often!

—**DOLLY CROGHAN** MEAD, NE

PREP: 35 MIN. + RISING • **BAKE:** 20 MIN.
MAKES: 12 SERVINGS

- 4½ cups all-purpose flour, divided
- ¼ cup sugar
- 2 packages (¼ ounce each) active dry yeast
- 1 teaspoon salt
- ¾ cup milk
- ½ cup water
- ½ cup shortening
- 2 large eggs

FILLING

- 2 pounds lean ground beef (90% lean)
- 2 medium onions, chopped
- 4 cups chopped cabbage
- 2 teaspoons seasoned salt
- 1 teaspoon garlic powder
- 1 teaspoon pepper

1. Place 1¾ cups flour, sugar, yeast and salt in a large bowl. Heat the milk, water and shortening to 120°-130°. Pour over flour mixture; add eggs. Beat with an electric mixer on low speed until blended. Beat 3 additional minutes on high. Stir in remaining flour; knead until smooth and elastic, about 6-8 minutes.
2. Place dough in a greased bowl; cover and let rise in a warm place until doubled, about 1 hour.
3. Meanwhile, in a large skillet, cook beef and onions over medium heat until meat is no longer pink; drain. Add the cabbage, seasoned salt, garlic powder and pepper; cook until cabbage is wilted.
4. Punch the dough down; divide into 12 portions and cover with plastic wrap. Working with one piece at a time, roll into a 6-in. square. Place ¾ cup meat mixture in the center of each square. Fold dough over filling, forming a rectangle. Pinch edges tightly to seal and place on greased baking sheets.
5. Bake at 350° for 18-20 minutes or until golden brown. Serve hot.

TURKEY GYROS

FAST FIX ▸
TURKEY GYROS

Greek seasoning, feta cheese and cucumber sauce give my lightened-up gyros an authentic taste. Instead of feta cheese, we sometimes use cheddar or Monterey Jack.

—**DONNA GARVIN** GLENS FALLS, NY

START TO FINISH: 25 MIN.
MAKES: 4 SERVINGS

- 1 medium cucumber, peeled
- ⅔ cup reduced-fat sour cream
- ¼ cup finely chopped onion
- 2 teaspoons dill weed
- 2 teaspoons lemon juice
- 1 teaspoon olive oil
- ½ pound turkey breast tenderloin, cut into ¼-inch slices
- 1½ teaspoons salt-free Greek seasoning
- 8 thin tomato slices
- 4 pita breads (6 inches), warmed
- 1½ cups shredded lettuce
- 2 tablespoons crumbled feta cheese

1. Finely chop one-third of the cucumber; place in a small bowl. Toss with sour cream, onion, dill and lemon juice. Thinly slice remaining cucumber.
2. In a nonstick skillet, heat oil over medium-high heat. Add turkey; cook and stir 5-7 minutes or until no longer pink. Sprinkle with Greek seasoning.
3. Serve turkey, tomato and sliced cucumber on pita breads. Top with lettuce, cheese and sauce.

TO MAKE YOUR OWN SALT-FREE GREEK SEASONING *In a small bowl, combine 1½ teaspoon dried oregano; 1 teaspoon each dried mint and dried thyme; ½ teaspoon each dried basil, dried marjoram and dried minced onion; and ¼ teaspoon dried minced garlic. Store airtight in a cool dry place for up to 6 months. Makes: 2 tablespoons.*

★ ★ ★ ★ ★ **5 STAR TIP**

To quickly get finely chopped onions, run a pizza cutter back and forth over sliced onions on your cutting board.

—**HAZEL G.** SPRING HILL, FL

EASY CHICKEN CORN CHOWDER

I often play around with ingredients in my pantry instead of running to the store when I haven't planned dinner. This was a happy experiment. You can always scale back on the bacon if you want, but it's so good with it!

—**BARBARA BANSKI** FENTON, MI

START TO FINISH: 30 MIN.
MAKES: 4 SERVINGS

- 2 tablespoons butter
- 1 small onion, finely chopped
- 1 celery rib, finely chopped
- 1 small sweet red pepper, finely chopped
- 2 cans (14¾ ounces each) cream-style corn
- 1½ cups chopped cooked chicken
- 1 can (12 ounces) reduced-fat evaporated milk
- 1 teaspoon chicken bouillon granules
- ½ teaspoon pepper
- 8 bacon strips, cooked and crumbled

1. In a large saucepan, heat butter over medium-high heat. Add onion, celery and red pepper; cook and stir 6-8 minutes or until tender.
2. Stir in corn, chicken, milk, bouillon and pepper; heat through, stirring occasionally (do not boil). Top servings with bacon.

CRISPY PITA BLT'S

Pack this sandwich full of fresh produce from your garden or the farmers market. You'll wow lunch guests with just-picked flavor.

—**MARY MILLER** POPLARVILLE, MS

PREP: 35 MIN. • **BAKE:** 15 MIN.
MAKES: 4 SERVINGS (2 PITA HALVES)

- ⅓ cup mayonnaise
- 1 garlic clove, minced
- ¼ teaspoon grated lemon peel
- ¼ cup all-purpose flour
- ¾ cup fat-free milk
- 1 cup panko (Japanese) bread crumbs

EASY CHICKEN CORN CHOWDER

- 2 medium yellow summer squash, cut into ¼-inch slices
- 2 jalapeno peppers, seeds removed and cut into ¼-inch slices
  Cooking spray
- 8 pita pocket halves
- 8 romaine leaves
- 8 slices tomato
- 16 cooked bacon strips, halved

1. In a small bowl, mix the mayonnaise, garlic and lemon peel. Cover and chill until serving.
2. Place flour, milk and bread crumbs in three separate shallow bowls. Coat squash and jalapeno slices with flour, then dip in milk and coat with bread crumbs. Place on baking sheets coated with cooking spray. Spritz vegetables with additional cooking spray.
3. Bake at 475° for 12-14 minutes or until golden brown, turning once.
4. Spread mayonnaise mixture inside pita halves; fill with lettuce, tomatoes, bacon and breaded vegetables. Serve immediately.

SUPER-DUPER TUNA SANDWICHES

If you pack this sandwich for a brown-bag lunch, keep the bread separate from the salad so it doesn't get soggy. You can also try serving the tuna salad with crackers, as a wrap or on lettuce.

—**RENEE BARTOLOMEO** INDIANOLA, IA

START TO FINISH: 15 MIN.
MAKES: 4 SERVINGS

- 2 cans (5 ounces each) light water-packed tuna, drained and flaked
- ⅓ cup shredded peeled apple
- ⅓ cup finely shredded cabbage
- ⅓ cup finely shredded carrot
- 3 tablespoons finely chopped celery
- 3 tablespoons finely chopped onion
- 3 tablespoons sweet pickle relish
- 2 tablespoons reduced-fat mayonnaise
- 8 slices whole wheat bread

In a large bowl, combine the first eight ingredients. Spread ½ cup tuna mixture over four slices of bread; top with the remaining bread slices.

QUICK PEPPERONI CALZONES

These toasty pockets come together in no time but taste as if they're from scratch. Take 'em to the next level with Parmesan and herbs on top.

—**SHANNON ROUM** MILWAUKEE, WI

START TO FINISH: 30 MIN.
MAKES: 4 SERVINGS

- 1 cup chopped pepperoni
- ½ cup pasta sauce with meat
- ¼ cup shredded part-skim mozzarella cheese
- 1 loaf (1 pound) frozen bread dough, thawed
- 1 to 2 tablespoons 2% milk
- 1 tablespoon grated Parmesan cheese
- ½ teaspoon Italian seasoning, optional

1. Preheat oven to 350°. In a small bowl, mix the pepperoni, pasta sauce and mozzarella cheese.

2. On a lightly floured surface, divide dough into four portions. Roll each into a 6-in. circle; top each with a scant ⅓ cup pepperoni mixture. Fold dough over filling; pinch edges to seal. Place on a greased baking sheet.

3. Brush milk over tops; sprinkle with Parmesan cheese and, if desired, Italian seasoning. Bake 20-25 minutes or until golden brown.

☆ ☆ ☆ ☆ ☆ **READER REVIEW**

"Delicious! I made these for my parents and family of 6. I used a breadmaker to make calzone dough. Besides the pepperoni filling, we also did pineapple and Canadian bacon. We will be making these a lot!"

POWELLCOU TASTEOFHOME.COM

QUICK PEPPERONI
CALZONES

GRANDMA'S SEAFOOD CHOWDER

My grandmother makes chowder every year for Christmas morning. But you can enjoy this satisfying recipe anytime.

—MELISSA OBERNESSER UTICA, NY

PREP: 15 MIN. • **COOK:** 25 MIN.
MAKES: 10 SERVINGS (3¾ QUARTS)

- 3 tablespoons plus ¼ cup butter, divided
- 1 pound sliced fresh mushrooms
- ⅓ cup all-purpose flour
- 1 teaspoon salt
- ⅛ teaspoon pepper
- 4 cups half-and-half cream
- 1½ cups 2% milk
- 1 pound haddock fillets, skin removed, cut into 1-inch pieces
- 1 pound uncooked medium shrimp, peeled and deveined
- 2 cups frozen peas (about 10 ounces)
- ¾ cup shredded cheddar cheese
- 1 cup lump crabmeat (about 5 ounces), drained
- 1 jar (4 ounces) diced pimientos, drained
- 1 teaspoon paprika

1. In a 6-qt. stockpot, heat 3 tablespoons butter over medium-high heat. Add mushrooms; cook and stir 8-10 minutes or until tender. Remove from pot.

2. In same pot, heat remaining butter over medium heat. Stir in flour, salt and pepper until smooth; gradually whisk in cream and milk. Bring to a boil, stirring constantly; cook and stir 2-3 minutes or until thickened.

3. Stir in the haddock, shrimp, peas and sauteed mushrooms; cook 5-7 minutes or until fish just begins to flake easily with a fork and shrimp turn pink. Add cheese, crab and pimientos; stir gently until cheese is melted. Sprinkle the servings with paprika.

FAST FIX >
HEARTY CHICKEN & WILD RICE SOUP

Garlic and herb cream cheese adds subtle notes of flavor to this creamy, hearty soup. On a chilly day—or any day—it's like having a bowlful of comfort.

—SHELISA TERRY HENDERSON, NV

START TO FINISH: 25 MIN.
MAKES: 6 SERVINGS (2¼ QUARTS)

- 1 package (6.2 ounces) fast-cooking long grain and wild rice mix
- 2 cans (10¾ ounces each) condensed cream of chicken and mushroom soup, undiluted
- 3 cups 2% milk
- 2 packages (6 ounces each) ready-to-use grilled chicken breast strips
- 2 cups frozen California-blend vegetables, thawed and coarsely chopped
- ¾ cup spreadable garlic and herb cream cheese

Prepare rice mix according to package directions using a Dutch oven. Stir in the remaining ingredients; heat through.

⑤INGREDIENTS FAST FIX >
ORANGE TURKEY CROISSANTS

Here's an easy, amazing sandwich that feels special. Sweet orange and crunchy pecans make it truly delicious. The best part? You need only five ingredients.

—JENNIFER MOORE CENTERVILLE, IA

START TO FINISH: 10 MIN.
MAKES: 6 SERVINGS

- 6 tablespoons spreadable cream cheese
- 6 tablespoons orange marmalade
- 6 croissants, split
- ½ cup chopped pecans
- 1 pound thinly sliced deli turkey

Spread cream cheese and marmalade onto the bottom half of croissants. Sprinkle with pecans. Top with turkey; replace tops.

ROASTED TOMATO AND PEPPER SOUP

You'll want to capture everything the roasted tomatoes, pepper, onion and garlic have to offer in this colorful soup. Add cubed hard bread pieces to soak up some of the soup.

—**DEBBY HARDEN** LANSING, MI

PREP: 45 MIN. • **COOK:** 45 MIN.
MAKES: 4 SERVINGS

- 2 **pounds plum tomatoes, halved lengthwise**
- 2 **medium sweet red peppers, quartered and seeded**
- 2 **medium onions, finely chopped**
- 2 **tablespoons olive oil**
- 3 **garlic cloves, minced**
- 2 **teaspoons ground cumin**
- 1 **teaspoon ground coriander**
- 1 **carton (32 ounces) reduced-sodium chicken broth**
- 3 **slices day-old French bread (1 inch thick), crusts removed and cubed**
- 1 **tablespoon balsamic vinegar**
- ¼ **teaspoon salt**
- ¼ **teaspoon pepper**
  Shaved Parmesan cheese

1. Place tomatoes and peppers, cut side down, in a 15x10x1-in. baking pan. Bake at 425° for 20 minutes. Turn tomatoes and peppers; bake 10-15 minutes longer or until skins are blistered and blackened.

2. Immediately place peppers and tomatoes in a large bowl; cover and let stand for 10 minutes. Peel off and discard skins; coarsely chop tomatoes and peppers.

3. In a large saucepan, saute onions in oil until tender. Add the garlic, cumin and coriander; saute 1 minute longer. Add the broth, tomatoes and peppers. Bring to a boil. Reduce heat; simmer, uncovered, for 30 minutes.

4. Stir in the bread, vinegar, salt and pepper; heat through. Sprinkle servings with cheese.

ROASTED TOMATO AND PEPPER SOUP

TURKEY & SWISS BISCUIT SLIDERS

I love to come up with new recipe ideas; I'm always experimenting. One of my favorite things to make is buttermilk biscuits, and I created this sandwich combo to perfectly complement the homemade biscuits.
—CINDY ESPOSITO BLOOMFIELD, NJ

PREP: 35 MIN. + RISING • **BAKE:** 10 MIN.
MAKES: 16 SERVINGS

- 1 package (¼ ounce) active dry yeast
- ⅔ cup warm buttermilk (110° to 115°)
- 2 tablespoons warm water (110° to 115°)
- 2 cups bread flour
- 3 tablespoons sugar
- 1½ teaspoons baking powder
- ½ teaspoon salt
- ½ cup shortening
- ¾ pound thinly sliced deli smoked turkey
- ½ pound sliced Swiss cheese
  Dijon mustard, optional

1. In a small bowl, dissolve yeast in warm buttermilk and water. Place flour, sugar, baking powder and salt in a food processor; pulse until blended. Add shortening; pulse until shortening is the size of peas. While processing, gradually add yeast mixture and process just until dough forms a ball.

2. Turn dough onto a lightly floured surface; knead 8-10 times. Pat or roll to ½-in. thickness; cut with a floured 2-in. biscuit cutter. Place 2 in. apart on greased baking sheets. Let rise until almost doubled, about 30 minutes.

3. Preheat oven to 425°. Bake biscuits 7-9 minutes or until golden brown. Remove to wire racks to cool slightly. Preheat broiler.

4. Split biscuits in half; place bottoms on greased baking sheets. Layer with the turkey and cheese. Broil 3-4 in. from the heat 2-3 minutes or until cheese is melted. Replace tops. If desired, serve with mustard.

SWEET & SPICY PULLED PORK SANDWICHES

SLOW COOKER
SWEET & SPICY PULLED PORK SANDWICHES

I threw some always-available condiments into my slow cooker with a pork roast to create this fantastic pulled pork. It has become a staple sandwich filler for large get-togethers. Serve with rolls, on top of toasted crostini, or as a filling for empanadas.
—LORI TERRY CHICAGO, IL

PREP: 30 MIN. • **COOK:** 8 HOURS
MAKES: 10 SERVINGS

- 2 medium onions, sliced (about 2 cups)
- 2 tablespoons brown sugar
- 1 tablespoon smoked paprika
- 1½ teaspoons salt
- ½ teaspoon pepper
- 1 boneless pork shoulder roast (4 to 5 pounds)
- ½ cup chicken or vegetable broth
- ¼ cup cider vinegar
- 3 tablespoons reduced-sodium soy sauce
- 3 tablespoons Worcestershire sauce
- 2 tablespoons Sriracha Asian hot chili sauce
- 1 tablespoon molasses
- 2 garlic cloves, minced
- 2 teaspoons Dijon mustard
- 3 cups coleslaw mix
- 3 tablespoons lime juice
- 10 kaiser or onion rolls, split

1. Place onions in a 4- or 5-qt. slow cooker. Mix brown sugar, paprika, salt and pepper; rub over roast. Place over the onions.

2. In a small bowl, mix the broth, vinegar, soy sauce, Worcestershire sauce, chili sauce, molasses, garlic and mustard; pour over roast. Cook, covered, on low 8-10 hours or until meat is tender.

3. Remove roast; cool slightly. Skim fat from cooking juices. In a small bowl, toss coleslaw mix with lime juice. Shred pork with two forks. Return pork to slow cooker; heat through. Serve on rolls with coleslaw.

SIDE DISHES, SALADS & MORE

★ ★ ★ ★ ★

A great side dish isn't simply a supporting actor—it may just steal the show! Choose from these top-rated recipes to complement your main course, or build a whole meal around them.

THREE-BEAN SALAD

Fresh herbs and cayenne pepper provide the punch in this marinated salad featuring fresh veggies and canned beans.

—**CAROL TUCKER** WOOSTER, OH

PREP: 20 MIN. + CHILLING
MAKES: 8 SERVINGS

- 1 can (15½ ounces) great northern beans, rinsed and drained
- 1 can (15 ounces) chickpeas, rinsed and drained
- 1 can (15 ounces) black beans, rinsed and drained
- 1 medium tomato, chopped
- 1 medium onion, chopped
- 1 celery rib, chopped
- ⅓ cup each chopped green, sweet red and yellow pepper
- ½ cup water
- 3 tablespoons minced fresh basil or 1 tablespoon dried basil
- 2 tablespoons minced fresh parsley
- 2 tablespoons lemon juice
- 2 tablespoons olive oil
- 1½ teaspoons minced fresh oregano or ½ teaspoon dried oregano
- ½ teaspoon salt
- ½ teaspoon pepper
- ¼ teaspoon cayenne pepper

In a large bowl, combine the beans, tomato, onion, celery and peppers. In a small bowl, whisk the remaining ingredients; gently stir into bean mixture. Cover and refrigerate for 4 hours, stirring occasionally.

★ ★ ★ ★ ★ **READER REVIEW**

"This is a great summer dish to bring to potluck dinners. It's refreshing and light and full of color. My family loves it and asks for more."

NANCYMAY70 TASTEOFHOME.COM

ITALIAN SALAD WITH
LEMON VINAIGRETTE

ITALIAN SALAD WITH LEMON VINAIGRETTE

For an Italian twist on salad, I mix greens with red onion, mushrooms, olives, pepperoncini, lemon juice and seasoning. Add tomatoes and carrots if you like.

—**DEBORAH LOOP** CLINTON TOWNSHIP, MI

START TO FINISH: 20 MIN.
MAKES: 8 SERVINGS (½ CUP VINAIGRETTE)

- 1 package (5 ounces) spring mix salad greens
- 1 small red onion, thinly sliced
- 1 cup sliced fresh mushrooms
- 1 cup assorted olives, pitted and coarsely chopped
- 8 pepperoncini
  Optional toppings: chopped tomatoes, shredded carrots and grated Parmesan cheese

VINAIGRETTE
- ⅓ cup extra virgin olive oil
- 3 tablespoons lemon juice
- 1 teaspoon Italian seasoning
- ¼ teaspoon salt
- ¼ teaspoon pepper

1. In a large bowl, combine the first five ingredients; toss lightly. If desired, add any of the optional toppings.
2. In a small bowl, whisk the vinaigrette ingredients until blended. Serve with the salad.

★ ★ ★ ★ ★ **READER REVIEW**

"We enjoyed this salad very much. I omitted the mushrooms and doubled the other ingredients. I used Castelvetrano olives. Delicious! It is definitely a keeper!"

ANNRMS TASTEOFHOME.COM

LUSCIOUS BLUEBERRY JAM

This perfectly spreadable jam boasts a beautiful dark color with a sweet, seasonal flavor.

—**KAREN HAEN** STURGEON BAY, WI

PREP: 20 MIN. • **COOK:** 20 MIN. + STANDING
MAKES: 8 CUPS

- 8 cups fresh blueberries
- 2 tablespoons lemon juice
- 1 package (1¾ ounces) powdered fruit pectin
- 7 cups sugar

1. Mash blueberries; transfer to a Dutch oven. Add lemon juice; stir in pectin. Bring to a full rolling boil over high heat, stirring constantly.
2. Stir in sugar; return to a full rolling boil. Boil for 1 minute, stirring constantly. Remove from the heat; skim off foam. Ladle into jars or freezer containers and cool to room temperature, about 1 hour.
3. Cover and let stand overnight or until set, but not longer than 24 hours. Refrigerate for up to 3 weeks or freeze for up to 12 months.

SAUSAGE & CORN BREAD DRESSING

At our house, we add sausage and a little steak sauce to our corn bread dressing. It warms us up on even the coldest days.

—**MANDY NALL** MONTGOMERY, AL

PREP: 30 MIN. • **BAKE:** 40 MIN.
MAKES: 12 SERVINGS

- 1 package (19½ ounces) Italian turkey sausage links, casings removed
- 4 medium onions, chopped (about 3 cups)
- ½ cup chopped celery
- 6 cups cubed day-old white or French bread
- 6 cups coarsely crumbled corn bread
- 2 large eggs
- 2 tablespoons steak sauce
- 2 teaspoons onion salt
- 2 teaspoons poultry seasoning
- 2 teaspoons dried parsley flakes
- 1 teaspoon garlic powder
- 1 teaspoon baking powder
- 2½ to 3 cups reduced-sodium chicken broth

1. Preheat oven to 350°. In a 6-qt. stockpot, cook sausage over medium heat for 6-8 minutes or until no longer pink, breaking into crumbles. Remove with a slotted spoon, reserving the drippings in the pot.
2. Add onions and celery to drippings; cook and stir for 6-8 minutes or until tender. Remove from heat; stir in sausage. Add cubed bread and corn bread; toss to combine.
3. In a small bowl, whisk eggs, steak sauce, seasonings and baking powder until blended; stir into the bread mixture. Stir in enough broth to reach desired moistness.
4. Transfer to a greased 13x9-in. or 3-qt. baking dish. Bake 40-50 minutes or until lightly browned.

BAKED PARMESAN BREADED SQUASH

Yellow summer squash crisps beautifully when baked. You don't have to turn the pieces, but do keep an eye on them.

—**DEBI MITCHELL** FLOWER MOUND, TX

PREP: 20 MIN. • **BAKE:** 20 MIN.
MAKES: 6 SERVINGS

- 4 cups thinly sliced yellow summer squash (3 medium)
- 3 tablespoons olive oil
- ½ teaspoon salt
- ½ teaspoon pepper
- ⅛ teaspoon cayenne pepper
- ¾ cup panko (Japanese) bread crumbs
- ¾ cup grated Parmesan cheese

1. Preheat oven to 450°. Place squash in a large bowl. Add olive oil and seasonings; toss to coat.
2. In a shallow bowl, mix bread crumbs and cheese. Dip squash in the crumb mixture to coat both sides, patting to help the coating adhere. Place on parchment paper-lined baking sheets. Bake 20-25 minutes or until golden brown, rotating pans halfway through baking.

**LOADED
SMASHED
POTATOES**

FAST FIX ▶

BRUSSELS SPROUTS & KALE SAUTE

This colorful side dish is filled with healthy greens. The crispy salami, my kid's favorite ingredient, makes it over-the-top delicious.
—**JENNIFER MCNABB** BRENTWOOD, TN

START TO FINISH: 30 MIN.
MAKES: 12 SERVINGS (½ CUP EACH)

- ¼ **pound thinly sliced hard salami, cut into ¼-inch strips**
- 1½ **teaspoons olive oil**
- 2 **tablespoons butter**
- 2 **pounds fresh Brussels sprouts, thinly sliced**
- 2 **cups shredded fresh kale**
- 1 **large onion, finely chopped**
- ½ **teaspoon kosher salt**
- ⅛ **teaspoon cayenne pepper**
- ¼ **teaspoon coarsely ground pepper**
- 1 **garlic clove, minced**
- ½ **cup chicken broth**
- ½ **cup chopped walnuts**
- 1 **tablespoon balsamic vinegar**

1. In a Dutch oven, cook and stir the salami in oil over medium-high heat for 3-5 minutes or until crisp. Remove to paper towels with a slotted spoon; reserve drippings in pan.
2. Add butter to the drippings; heat over medium-high heat. Add Brussels sprouts, kale, onion, salt, cayenne and black pepper; cook and stir until the vegetables are crisp-tender. Add garlic; cook for 1 minute longer.
3. Stir in the broth; bring to a boil. Reduce heat; cover and cook 4-5 minutes or until the Brussels sprouts are tender. Stir in walnuts and vinegar. Serve with salami strips.

★ ★ ★ ★ ★ 5 STAR TIP

If you're using your oven for your entree, plan your hot side dishes accordingly. Choose a side dish that can be prepared on the stovetop or in a slow cooker. If you do need to use the oven, choose a recipe that cooks at the same temperature as your main course, or pick a dish that can be prepared ahead and heated just before serving.

LOADED SMASHED POTATOES

If mashed potatoes are a must at your family Thanksgiving, then why not go all out with the works? I love garlic, onions and bacon—this dish has all three!
—**KATHY HARDING** RICHMOND, MO

PREP: 40 MIN. • **BAKE:** 10 MIN.
MAKES: 15 SERVINGS

- 2 **whole garlic bulbs**
- 1 **tablespoon canola oil**
- 8 **bacon strips**
- 3 **green onions, chopped**
- 4 **pounds small red potatoes**
- 1 **container (16 ounces) sour cream**
- 1½ **cups (6 ounces) shredded cheddar cheese, divided**
- ⅓ **cup butter, softened**
- ¼ **cup 2% milk**
- ½ **teaspoon salt**
- ¼ **teaspoon pepper**
  Minced chives, optional

1. Remove papery outer skin from garlic (do not peel or separate the cloves). Cut tops off garlic bulbs. Brush with oil. Wrap each bulb in heavy-duty foil.
2. Bake at 425° for 30-35 minutes or until softened. Cool for 10 minutes.
3. Meanwhile, in a large skillet, cook bacon over medium heat until crisp. Remove to paper towels; drain, reserving 2 tablespoons drippings. In the same skillet, cook onions in reserved drippings for 2 minutes or until tender; set aside. Crumble bacon.
4. Place the red potatoes in a large saucepan and cover with water. Bring to a boil. Reduce heat; cover and cook 10-15 minutes or until tender. Drain and transfer to a large bowl.
5. Mash the potatoes. Squeeze the softened garlic over top. Stir in bacon, onions with drippings, sour cream, 1 cup cheese, butter, milk, salt and pepper; combine. Spoon the mixture into a greased 13x9-in. baking dish; top with remaining cheese.
6. Bake, uncovered, at 350° for 10-15 minutes or until the cheese is melted. Garnish with chives if desired.

VEGGIE CHOPPED SALAD

My husband's aunt gave me this recipe in 1987, and it's been a staple at our house ever since. I like to make it a day ahead because some time in the fridge makes it even better. Be sure to save yourself some leftovers, too.
—**MADELINE ETZKORN** BURIEN, WA

START TO FINISH: 25 MIN.
MAKES: 12 SERVINGS (¾ CUP EACH)

- 3 **cups finely chopped fresh broccoli**
- 3 **cups finely chopped cauliflower**
- 3 **cups finely chopped celery**
- 2 **cups frozen peas (about 8 ounces), thawed**
- 6 **bacon strips, cooked and crumbled**
- 1⅓ **cups mayonnaise**
- ¼ **cup sugar**
- 2 **tablespoons grated Parmesan cheese**
- 1 **tablespoon cider vinegar**
- ¼ **teaspoon salt**
- ¾ **cup salted peanuts**

In a large bowl, combine the first five ingredients. In a small bowl, mix the mayonnaise, sugar, cheese, vinegar and salt until blended. Add to the salad and toss to coat. Just before serving, stir in peanuts. Refrigerate any leftovers.

⑤ INGREDIENTS **FAST FIX ▶**

BACON-TOMATO SALAD

We love this wonderful salad that tastes like a piled-high BLT without the time or effort! Plus, you can make it hours ahead and keep it in the fridge until serving time.
—**DENISE THURMAN** COLUMBIA, MO

START TO FINISH: 15 MIN.
MAKES: 6 SERVINGS

- 1 **package (12 ounces) iceberg lettuce blend**
- 2 **cups grape tomatoes, halved**
- ¾ **cup coleslaw salad dressing**
- ¾ **cup shredded cheddar cheese**
- 12 **bacon strips, cooked and crumbled**

In a large bowl, combine lettuce blend and tomatoes. Drizzle with dressing; sprinkle with cheese and bacon.

VEGGIE CHOPPED SALAD

BACON-TOMATO SALAD

LIME AND SESAME GRILLED EGGPLANT

When I lived in Greece, I fell in love with eggplant. My recipe's seasonings have an Asian theme, but the dish still makes me think Greek.
—**ALLYSON MEYLER** GREENSBORO, NC

START TO FINISH: 20 MIN.
MAKES: 6 SERVINGS

- 3 tablespoons lime juice
- 1 tablespoon sesame oil
- 1½ teaspoons reduced-sodium soy sauce
- 1 garlic clove, minced
- ½ teaspoon grated fresh gingerroot or ¼ teaspoon ground ginger
- ½ teaspoon salt
- ⅛ teaspoon pepper
- 1 medium eggplant (1¼ pounds), cut lengthwise into ½-inch slices
- 2 teaspoons honey
- ⅛ teaspoon crushed red pepper flakes
  Thinly sliced green onion and sesame seeds

1. In a small bowl, whisk the first seven ingredients until blended; brush 2 tablespoons of the lime-juice mixture over both sides of eggplant slices. Grill, covered, over medium heat 4-6 minutes on each side or until tender.
2. Transfer the eggplant to a serving plate. Stir honey and pepper flakes into the remaining juice mixture; drizzle over eggplant. Sprinkle with green onion and sesame seeds.

★ ★ ★ ★ ★ **READER REVIEW**

"I'm an eggplant lover and found this excellent. Just enough spice, balanced with a touch of sweetness."

AUG2295 TASTEOFHOME.COM

EDDIE'S FAVORITE FIESTA CORN

EDDIE'S FAVORITE FIESTA CORN

When sweet corn is available, I love making this splurge of a side dish. Frozen corn works, but taste as you go and add sugar if needed.
—**ANTHONY BOLTON** BELLEVUE, NE

PREP: 15 MIN. • **COOK:** 25 MIN.
MAKES: 8 SERVINGS

- ½ pound bacon strips, chopped
- 5 cups fresh or frozen super sweet corn
- 1 medium sweet red pepper, finely chopped
- 1 medium sweet yellow pepper, finely chopped
- 1 package (8 ounces) reduced-fat cream cheese
- ½ cup half-and-half cream
- 1 can (4 ounces) chopped green chilies, optional
- 2 teaspoons sugar
- 1 teaspoon pepper
- ¼ teaspoon salt

1. In a 6-qt. stockpot, cook bacon over medium heat until crisp, stirring occasionally. Remove with a slotted spoon; drain on paper towels. Discard drippings, reserving 1 tablespoon in pan.
2. Add corn, red pepper and yellow pepper to drippings; cook and stir over medium-high heat for 5-6 minutes or until tender. Stir in remaining ingredients until blended; bring to a boil. Reduce heat; simmer, covered, for 8-10 minutes or until thickened.

SPRING GREEN RISOTTO

Once a week, I create a new recipe for my blog, An Officer and a Vegan. I first made this risotto when I needed something cheerful and satisfying. It would be fantastic with asparagus, zucchini or summer squash, but use whatever veggies are in season.

—DEANNA MCDONALD GRAND RAPIDS, MI

PREP: 15 MIN. • **COOK:** 30 MIN.
MAKES: 8 SERVINGS

- 1 **carton (32 ounces) vegetable stock**
- 1 **to 1½ cups water**
- 1 **tablespoon olive oil**
- 2 **cups sliced fresh mushrooms**
- 1 **medium onion, chopped**
- 1½ **cups uncooked arborio rice**
- 2 **garlic cloves, minced**
- ½ **cup white wine or additional vegetable stock**
- 1 **teaspoon dried thyme**
- 3 **cups fresh baby spinach**
- 1 **cup frozen peas**
- 3 **tablespoons grated Parmesan cheese**
- 1 **tablespoon red wine vinegar**
- ½ **teaspoon salt**
- ¼ **teaspoon pepper**

1. In a large saucepan, bring stock and water to a simmer; keep hot. In a Dutch oven, heat oil over medium-high heat. Add mushrooms and onion; cook and stir for 5-7 minutes or until tender. Add rice and garlic; cook and stir for 1-2 minutes or until rice is coated.

2. Stir in wine and thyme. Reduce heat to maintain a simmer; cook and stir until wine is absorbed. Add hot stock mixture, ½ cup at a time, cooking and stirring after each addition until stock has been absorbed; continue until rice is tender but firm to the bite and risotto is creamy. Stir in the remaining ingredients; heat through. Serve immediately.

REFRIGERATOR JALAPENO DILL PICKLES

REFRIGERATOR JALAPENO DILL PICKLES

I'm passionate about making pickles; my husband is passionate about eating them. He's too impatient to let them cure on the shelf, so I found this quick recipe to make him happy. Add hotter peppers if you like the heat.

—ANNIE JENSEN ROSEAU, MN

PREP: 20 MIN. + CHILLING
MAKES: ABOUT 4 DOZEN PICKLE SPEARS

- 3 **pounds pickling cucumbers (about 12)**
- 1 **small onion, halved and sliced**
- ¼ **cup snipped fresh dill**
- 1 **to 2 jalapeno peppers, sliced**
- 3 **garlic cloves, minced**
- 2½ **cups water**
- 2½ **cups cider vinegar**
- ⅓ **cup canning salt**
- ⅓ **cup sugar**

1. Cut each cucumber lengthwise into four spears. In a very large bowl, combine cucumbers, onion, dill, jalapenos and garlic. In a large saucepan, combine the water, vinegar, salt and sugar. Bring to a boil; cook and stir just until salt and sugar are dissolved. Pour over the cucumber mixture; cool.

2. Cover tightly and refrigerate for at least 24 hours. Store in the refrigerator for up to 2 months.

NOTE *Wear disposable gloves when cutting hot peppers; the oils can burn skin. Avoid touching your face.*

SPRING GREEN RISOTTO

ROASTED CABBAGE & ONIONS

I roast veggies to bring out their sweetness, and it works wonders with onions and cabbage. The puckery vinegar-mustard sauce makes this appetizing dish similar to a slaw.

—ANN SHEEHY LAWRENCE, MA

PREP: 10 MIN. • **COOK:** 30 MIN. + STANDING
MAKES: 6 SERVINGS

- 1 medium head cabbage (about 2 pounds), coarsely chopped
- 2 large onions, chopped
- ¼ cup olive oil
- ¾ teaspoon salt
- ¾ teaspoon pepper
- 3 tablespoons minced fresh chives
- 3 tablespoons minced fresh tarragon

DRESSING
- 2 tablespoons white balsamic vinegar or white wine vinegar
- 2 tablespoons olive oil
- 2 tablespoons Dijon mustard
- 1 tablespoon lemon juice
- ½ teaspoon salt
- ½ teaspoon pepper

1. Preheat oven to 450°. Place cabbage and onions in a large bowl. Drizzle with oil; sprinkle with salt and pepper and toss to coat. Transfer to a shallow roasting pan, spreading evenly. Roast for 30-35 minutes or until vegetables are tender and lightly browned, stirring halfway.
2. Transfer the cabbage mixture to a large bowl. Add chives and tarragon; toss to combine. In a small bowl, whisk dressing ingredients until blended. Drizzle over cabbage mixture; toss to coat. Let stand 10 minutes to allow flavors to blend. Serve warm or at room temperature.

HOW TO REMOVE THE CORE FROM CABBAGE

Cut cabbage in half or into quarters. Use a sharp knife to make a V-shaped cut around the core; remove it.

DAD'S GREEK SALAD

FAST FIX
DAD'S GREEK SALAD

The heart of a Greek salad is the olives, feta, cucumbers and tomatoes. Dress it with olive oil and vinegar, then add more olives and more cheese!

—ARGE SALVATORI WALDWICK, NJ

START TO FINISH: 20 MIN.
MAKES: 8 SERVINGS

- 4 large tomatoes, seeded and coarsely chopped
- 2½ cups (about 6) thinly sliced English cucumbers
- 1 small red onion, halved and thinly sliced
- ¼ cup olive oil
- 3 tablespoons red wine vinegar
- ¼ teaspoon salt
- ⅛ teaspoon pepper
- ¼ teaspoon dried oregano, optional
- ¾ cup pitted Greek olives
- ¾ cup (3 ounces) crumbled feta cheese

Place tomatoes, cucumbers and onion in a large bowl. In a small bowl, whisk oil, vinegar, salt, pepper and, if desired, oregano until blended. Drizzle over salad; toss to coat. Top with olives and cheese.

⑤ INGREDIENTS
GARLIC-CHIVE BAKED FRIES

Almost no one can resist golden-brown fries seasoned with garlic and fresh chives. They are especially great alongside a juicy steak.

—STEVE WESTPHAL WIND LAKE, WI

PREP: 15 MIN. • **BAKE:** 20 MIN.
MAKES: 4 SERVINGS

- 4 medium russet potatoes
- 1 tablespoon olive oil
- 4 teaspoons dried minced chives
- ½ teaspoon salt
- ½ teaspoon garlic powder
- ¼ teaspoon pepper

1. Preheat oven to 450°. Cut potatoes into ¼-in. julienne strips. Rinse well and pat dry.
2. Transfer the potatoes to a large bowl. Drizzle with oil; sprinkle with remaining ingredients. Toss to coat. Arrange in a single layer in two 15x10x1-in. baking pans coated with cooking spray.
3. Bake 20-25 minutes or until lightly browned, turning once.

BLT TWICE-BAKED POTATOES

Two favorites go together in this hearty dish: BLTs and twice-baked potatoes. I like to serve them alongside juicy grilled steaks or tender barbecued chicken.

—**MARY SHENK** DEKALB, IL

PREP: 25 MIN. • **BAKE:** 15 MIN.
MAKES: 8 SERVINGS

- **4 medium potatoes (about 8 ounces each)**
- **½ cup mayonnaise**
- **1 cup (4 ounces) shredded cheddar cheese**
- **8 bacon strips, cooked and crumbled**
- **⅓ cup oil-packed sun-dried tomatoes, patted dry and chopped**
- **1 green onion, thinly sliced**
- **½ teaspoon salt**
- **¼ teaspoon pepper**
- **1 cup shredded lettuce**

1. Preheat oven to 400°. Scrub potatoes; pierce several times with a fork. Place on a microwave-safe plate. Microwave, uncovered, on high for 12-15 minutes or until tender, turning once.

2. When cool enough to handle, cut each potato lengthwise in half. Scoop out pulp, leaving ¼-in.-thick shells. In a small bowl, mash the pulp with mayonnaise, adding cheese, bacon, tomatoes, green onion, salt and pepper.

3. Spoon the pulp mixture into the potato shells. Place on a baking sheet. Bake for 12-15 minutes or until heated through. Sprinkle with lettuce.

BLT TWICE-BAKED POTATOES

FAST FIX ▶

BUTTERY-HORSERADISH CORN ON THE COB

For a July Fourth barbecue, I whipped up a butter and horseradish topping for grilled corn. People actually formed a line to get seconds!

—TRISH LOEWEN BAKERSFIELD, CA

START TO FINISH: 30 MIN.
MAKES: 12 SERVINGS

- ¾ cup butter, softened
- ¼ cup shredded pepper jack cheese
- ¼ cup prepared horseradish
- 1 tablespoon dried parsley flakes
- 3 teaspoons salt
- 2 teaspoons balsamic vinegar
- ½ teaspoon pepper
- ¼ teaspoon dried thyme
- 12 medium ears sweet corn, husks removed

1. In a small bowl, mix the first eight ingredients until blended; spread over corn. Wrap each ear with a piece of heavy-duty foil (about 14 in. square), sealing tightly.

2. Grill corn, covered, over medium heat for 15-20 minutes or until tender, turning occasionally. Open foil carefully to allow steam to escape.

ZESTY COLESLAW

This simple slaw tastes best when it's refrigerated for at least one hour. The mixture tends to get creamier as it sits.

—MICHELLE GAUER SPICER, MN

PREP: 15 MIN. + CHILLING
MAKES: 12 SERVINGS (⅔ CUP EACH)

- 1 cup mayonnaise
- ⅓ cup sugar
- 3 tablespoons cider vinegar
- 1 teaspoon seasoned salt
- ¾ teaspoon pepper
- ½ teaspoon celery seed
- 2 packages (14 ounces each) coleslaw mix
- 1 small sweet red pepper, chopped
- ½ cup thinly sliced sweet onion

In a large bowl, mix the first six ingredients. Add coleslaw mix, red pepper and onion; toss to coat. Refrigerate at least 1 hour before serving.

BUTTERY-HORSERADISH CORN ON THE COB

GRANDMA'S CRANBERRY STUFF

What tastes better than turkey and cranberries at Thanksgiving? The classic pairing gets even better with my grandma's signature cranberry dish. Your friends and family will love it!

—CATHERINE CASSIDY MILWAUKEE, WI

PREP: 10 MIN.
MAKES: 3 CUPS

- 1 medium navel orange
- 1 package (12 ounces) fresh or frozen cranberries, thawed
- 1 cup sugar
- 1 cup chopped walnuts, toasted

Cut unpeeled orange into wedges, removing any seeds, and place in a food processor. Add cranberries and sugar; pulse until chopped. Add walnuts; pulse just until combined.
NOTE *To toast nuts, bake in a shallow pan in a 350° oven for 5-10 minutes or cook in a skillet over low heat until lightly browned, stirring occasionally.*

HERBED BUTTERNUT SQUASH

We always keep butternut squash on hand in the cooler months. We particularly enjoy it grilled with a dash of oregano and thyme.

—JENN TIDWELL FAIR OAKS, CA

START TO FINISH: 25 MIN.
MAKES: 6 SERVINGS

- 1 medium butternut squash (about 3 pounds)
- 1 tablespoon olive oil
- 1½ teaspoons dried oregano
- 1 teaspoon dried thyme
- ½ teaspoon salt
- ¼ teaspoon pepper

Peel and cut squash crosswise into ½-in.-thick slices; remove and discard the seeds. In a large bowl, toss squash with the remaining ingredients. Grill, covered, over medium heat or broil 4 in. from heat 6-8 minutes on each side or until tender.

MICHIGAN CHERRY SALAD

This recipe reminds me what I love about my home state: apple picking with my children, buying greens at the farmers market and tasting cherries on vacations.

—JENNIFER GILBERT BRIGHTON, MI

START TO FINISH: 15 MIN.
MAKES: 8 SERVINGS

- 7 ounces fresh baby spinach (about 9 cups)
- 3 ounces spring mix salad greens (about 5 cups)
- 1 large apple, chopped
- ½ cup coarsely chopped pecans, toasted
- ½ cup dried cherries
- ¼ cup crumbled Gorgonzola cheese

DRESSING
- ¼ cup fresh raspberries
- ¼ cup red wine vinegar
- 3 tablespoons cider vinegar
- 3 tablespoons cherry preserves
- 1 tablespoon sugar
- 2 tablespoons olive oil

1. In a large bowl, combine the first six ingredients.
2. Place raspberries, vinegars, preserves and sugar in a blender. While processing, gradually add the oil in a steady stream. Drizzle over salad; toss to coat.
NOTE *To toast nuts, bake in a shallow pan in a 350° oven for 5-10 minutes or cook in a skillet over low heat until lightly browned, stirring occasionally.*

★ ★ ★ ★ ★ **READER REVIEW**

"I normally make all of my salad dressings and have never made one with berries in it. Brilliant idea. I substituted feta for the Gorgonzola, as I had it on hand. My dinner guests loved it. Great salad to add to my rotation."

RLCURRY1 TASTEOFHOME.COM

CRISPY SMASHED HERBED POTATOES

½ teaspoon sugar
¼ teaspoon dried oregano
3 large heirloom tomatoes, sliced
½ cup fresh basil leaves
⅓ cup pine nuts, toasted
3 tablespoons chopped red onion
2 ounces fresh goat cheese, crumbled

Place salad greens in a large bowl. In a small bowl, whisk oil, vinegar, mustard, garlic, sugar and oregano until blended. Pour over salad greens; toss to coat. Transfer to a large platter. Arrange tomato slices over greens. Top with basil, pine nuts, onion and cheese. Serve immediately.

NOTE *To toast nuts, bake in a shallow pan in a 350° oven for 5-10 minutes or cook in a skillet over low heat until lightly browned, stirring occasionally.*

LIME-HONEY FRUIT SALAD

Nothing is more refreshing to me than a seasonal fruit salad enhanced with this simple lime-honey dressing.
—VICTORIA SHEVLIN CAPE CORAL, FL

PREP: 20 MIN. + CHILLING
MAKES: 12 SERVINGS (¾ CUP EACH)

1 teaspoon cornstarch
¼ cup lime juice
¼ cup honey
½ teaspoon poppy seeds
3 medium Gala or Red Delicious apples, cubed
2 medium pears, cubed
2 cups seedless red grapes
2 cups green grapes

1. In a small microwave-safe bowl, combine cornstarch and lime juice until smooth. Microwave, uncovered, on high 20 seconds; stir. Cook 15 seconds longer; stir. Stir in honey and poppy seeds.
2. In a large bowl, combine the apples, pears and grapes. Pour the dressing over the fruit; toss to coat. Cover and refrigerate overnight.
NOTE *This recipe was tested in a 1,100-watt microwave.*

---

⑤INGREDIENTS
CRISPY SMASHED HERBED POTATOES

Golden brown and buttery, these spuds live up to their tantalizing name. A sprinkle of fresh herbs when they're hot out of the oven maximizes the flavor...and the pretty.
—ALTHEA DYE HOWARD, OH

PREP: 25 MIN. • **BAKE:** 20 MIN.
MAKES: 4 SERVINGS

12 small red potatoes (about 1½ pounds)
3 tablespoons olive oil
¼ cup butter, melted
¾ teaspoon salt
¼ teaspoon pepper
3 tablespoons minced fresh chives
1 tablespoon minced fresh parsley

1. Preheat oven to 450°. Place potatoes in a large saucepan; add water to cover. Bring to a boil. Reduce heat; cook, uncovered, 15-20 minutes or until tender. Drain.

2. Drizzle oil over the bottom of a 15x10x1-in. baking pan; arrange potatoes over oil. Using a potato masher, flatten potatoes to ½-in. thickness. Brush potatoes with butter; sprinkle with salt and pepper.
3. Roast 20-25 minutes or until golden brown. Sprinkle with chives and parsley.

FAST FIX
FRESH HEIRLOOM TOMATO SALAD

This tomato salad is a summertime must. The standout dressing takes the tasty ingredients to a brand-new level.
—TASTE OF HOME TEST KITCHEN

START TO FINISH: 20 MIN.
MAKES: 12 SERVINGS

1 package (5 ounces) spring mix salad greens
3 tablespoons olive oil
2 tablespoons balsamic vinegar
1 teaspoon Dijon mustard
1 garlic clove, minced

HOW TO PREP A PEPPER

Cut top and bottom off pepper and discard. Cut each side from pepper by slicing close to the center and then down. Scrape out seeds and discard.

Cut away any ribs.

Place skin side down on work surface and flatten slightly with your hand. Cut lengthwise into strips.

SWEET ONION & RED BELL PEPPER TOPPING

SLOW COOKER

SWEET ONION & RED BELL PEPPER TOPPING

As soon as the spring Vidalia onions hit the market, this is one of the first recipes I make. I use it on hot dogs, bruschetta, cream cheese and crackers. It is so versatile.

—**PAT HOCKETT** OCALA, FL

PREP: 20 MIN. • **COOK:** 4 HOURS
MAKES: 4 CUPS

- 4 **large sweet onions, thinly sliced (about 8 cups)**
- 4 **large sweet red peppers, thinly sliced (about 6 cups)**
- ½ **cup cider vinegar**
- ¼ **cup packed brown sugar**
- 2 **tablespoons canola oil**
- 2 **tablespoons honey**
- 2 **teaspoons celery seed**
- ¾ **teaspoon crushed red pepper flakes**
- ½ **teaspoon salt**

In a 5- or 6-qt. slow cooker, combine all ingredients. Cook, covered, on low for 4-5 hours or until the vegetables are tender. Serve with a slotted spoon.

PATIO PINTOS

Any time Mom had folks over for dinner, she made these pinto beans. One time, she made a batch for my cousin's birthday, and he ate the entire thing himself!

—**JOAN HALLFORD** NORTH RICHLAND HILLS, TX

PREP: 25 MIN. • **BAKE:** 1 HOUR
MAKES: 10 SERVINGS

- ½ **pound bacon strips, chopped**
- 1 **large onion, chopped**
- 2 **garlic cloves, minced**
- 6 **cans (15 ounces each) pinto beans, rinsed and drained**
- 4 **cans (8 ounces each) tomato sauce**
- 2 **cans (4 ounces each) chopped green chilies**
- ⅓ **cup packed brown sugar**
- 1 **teaspoon chili powder**
- ¾ **teaspoon salt**
- ½ **teaspoon dried oregano**
- ¼ **teaspoon pepper**

1. Preheat oven to 350°. In a Dutch oven, cook bacon over medium heat until crisp, stirring occasionally. Remove with a slotted spoon; drain on paper towels. Discard drippings; reserve 2 tablespoons in the pot.

2. Add onion to drippings; cook and stir over medium heat for 6-8 minutes or until tender. Add garlic; cook 1 minute longer. Stir in beans, tomato sauce, green chilies, brown sugar and seasonings. Sprinkle top with bacon. Bake, covered, 60-70 minutes or until heated through.

FREEZE OPTION *Freeze cooled bean mixture in freezer containers. To use, partially thaw in refrigerator overnight. Heat through in a saucepan, stirring occasionally and adding a little water if necessary.*

PESTO BUTTERMILK DRESSING

A good dressing is hard to beat; a great one is brilliant. We love this tangy blend of buttermilk and Greek yogurt.

—**LIZ BELLVILLE** HAVELOCK, NC

PREP: 10 MIN. + CHILLING
MAKES: 1¾ CUPS

- ⅔ **cup buttermilk**
- ½ **cup fat-free plain Greek yogurt**
- ½ **cup prepared pesto**
- ¼ **cup shredded Parmesan cheese**
- 1 **tablespoon white wine vinegar**
- 1 **tablespoon grated lemon peel**
- 1 **garlic clove, minced**
- ½ **teaspoon coarsely ground pepper**
- ⅛ **teaspoon salt**

Place all ingredients in a jar with a tight-fitting lid; shake well. Refrigerate for 1 hour. Just before serving, shake the dressing again.

GREAT GRAIN SALAD

I can't think of a better dish to round out a meal. My grain salad features some of the best nuts, seeds and fruits. Try adding grilled chicken to make it a meal on its own.

—RACHEL DUEKER GERVAIS, OR

PREP: 15 MIN. • **COOK:** 1 HOUR + CHILLING
MAKES: 12 SERVINGS (¾ CUP EACH)

- 3 cups water
- ½ cup medium pearl barley
- ½ cup uncooked wild rice
- ⅔ cup uncooked basmati rice
- ½ cup slivered almonds
- ½ cup sunflower kernels
- ½ cup salted pumpkin seeds or pepitas
- ½ cup each golden raisins, chopped dried apricots and dried cranberries
- ⅓ cup minced fresh parsley
- 4 teaspoons grated orange peel

VINAIGRETTE
- ⅔ cup walnut oil
- ⅔ cup raspberry vinegar
- 2 teaspoons orange juice
- 2 teaspoons pepper
- 1 teaspoon salt

1. In a large saucepan, bring water to a boil. Add barley and wild rice. Reduce heat; cover and simmer for 55-65 minutes or until tender. Meanwhile, cook basmati rice according to package directions. Cool barley and rices to room temperature.

2. In a large bowl, combine the almonds, sunflower kernels, pumpkin seeds, dried fruit, parsley and orange peel; add the barley and rice.

3. In a small bowl, whisk the vinaigrette ingredients. Pour over the salad and toss to coat. Cover and refrigerate for at least 2 hours.

★ ★ ★ ★ ★ **5 STAR TIP**

Wild rice and barley may become tender without absorbing all the cooking liquid—don't worry if you have liquid left in the pan! Just drain before serving or adding to your other recipe ingredients. Leftover wild rice and barley freeze well; defrost and reheat in the microwave for use in recipes calling for cooked rice or for a quick side dish.

WATERMELON & SPINACH SALAD

FAST FIX ▶
WATERMELON & SPINACH SALAD

Now's the perfect time to toss up my melon salad. You'd never expect it, but spinach is awesome here. Eat it, and feel cool on even the hottest days.

—MARJORIE AU HONOLULU, HI

START TO FINISH: 30 MIN.
MAKES: 8 SERVINGS

- ¼ cup rice vinegar or white wine vinegar
- 1 tablespoon grated lime peel
- 2 tablespoons lime juice
- 2 tablespoons canola oil
- 4 teaspoons minced fresh gingerroot
- 2 garlic cloves, minced
- ½ teaspoon salt
- ¼ teaspoon sugar
- ¼ teaspoon pepper

SALAD
- 4 cups fresh baby spinach or arugula
- 3 cups cubed seedless watermelon
- 2 cups cubed cantaloupe
- 2 cups cubed English cucumber
- ½ cup chopped fresh cilantro
- 2 green onions, chopped

In a small bowl, whisk the first nine ingredients. In a large bowl, combine the salad ingredients. Drizzle with dressing and toss to coat; serve immediately.

FAST FIX ▶
ZESTY GARLIC GREEN BEANS

If you're in charge of bringing a side dish to a party, change up the usual green bean casserole. These beans travel well, too.

—CHRISTINE BERGMAN SUWANEE, GA

START TO FINISH: 25 MIN.
MAKES: 10 SERVINGS

- 2 tablespoons oil from oil-packed sun-dried tomatoes
- 1 cup sliced sweet onion
- ½ cup oil-packed sun-dried tomatoes, chopped
- 3 garlic cloves, minced
- 1½ teaspoons lemon-pepper seasoning
- 2 packages (16 ounces each) frozen french-style green beans

1. In a Dutch oven, heat oil over medium heat. Add sliced onion; cook and stir for 3-4 minutes or until tender. Add the tomatoes, garlic and lemon pepper; cook and stir for 2 minutes longer.

2. Stir in frozen green beans; cook, covered for 7-9 minutes or until heated through, stirring occasionally. Uncover; cook for 2-3 minutes longer or until liquid is almost evaporated.

MAIN DISHES

★★★★★

Invite the family to the table tonight with a homemade dinner—it can be simple, you'll see! If you're searching for a comforting, satisfying entree for the whole family, look no further.

SASSY POT ROAST

We lost this recipe for several years, so it's even more special to us now that we found it again. I love walking into my home after a long day at the office and smelling this lovely pot roast.

—**SUSAN BURKETT** MONROEVILLE, PA

PREP: 15 MIN. • **COOK:** 8 HOURS
MAKES: 8 SERVINGS

- 1 **boneless beef chuck roast (2 pounds)**
- ½ **teaspoon salt**
- ½ **teaspoon pepper**
- 2 **teaspoons olive oil**
- 1 **large onion, chopped**
- 1 **can (8 ounces) tomato sauce**
- ¼ **cup water**
- ¼ **cup lemon juice**
- ¼ **cup cider vinegar**
- ¼ **cup ketchup**
- 2 **tablespoons brown sugar**
- 1 **tablespoon Worcestershire sauce**
- ½ **teaspoon ground mustard**
- ½ **teaspoon paprika**

1. Sprinkle beef with salt and pepper. In a large skillet, brown beef in oil on all sides; drain.
2. Transfer to a 4-qt. slow cooker. Sprinkle with onion. Combine the remaining ingredients; pour over meat. Cover and cook on low for 8-10 hours or until meat is tender. Skim fat. If desired, thicken cooking liquid.

★ ★ ★ ★ ★ **READER REVIEW**

"This pot roast was a great change from some other recipes. I added carrots during the last 5 hours of cooking—it turned out great and the carrots weren't mushy. I will definitely make this again."

JAIME1103 TASTEOFHOME.COM

APPLE ROASTED PORK WITH CHERRY BALSAMIC GLAZE

FAST FIX ▶

PINTO BEAN TOSTADAS

Ready-to-go pinto beans and crispy corn tortillas prove how easy it is to make a healthy meal. Sometimes I add some chopped leftover meat to the tostadas, but they're equally satisfying just as they are.

—LILY JULOW LAWRENCEVILLE, GA

START TO FINISH: 30 MIN.
MAKES: 6 SERVINGS

- ¼ **cup sour cream**
- ¾ **teaspoon grated lime peel**
- ¼ **teaspoon ground cumin**
- ½ **teaspoon salt, divided**
- 2 **tablespoons canola oil, divided**
- 2 **garlic cloves, minced**
- 2 **cans (15 ounces each) pinto beans, rinsed and drained**
- 1 **to 2 teaspoons hot pepper sauce**
- 1 **teaspoon chili powder**
- 6 **corn tortillas (6 inches)**
- 2 **cups shredded lettuce**
- ½ **cup salsa**
- ¾ **cup crumbled feta cheese or queso fresco**
  Lime wedges

APPLE ROASTED PORK WITH CHERRY BALSAMIC GLAZE

I added roasted apples, cherries and onions to turn ordinary pork into a brand-new dish. I haven't turned back since! There is a short time frame between caramelized onions and burnt ones, so pay close attention once they start cooking.

—JOSH DOWNEY MCHENRY, IL

PREP: 30 MIN. • **BAKE:** 50 MIN. + STANDING
MAKES: 8 SERVINGS

- 1 **boneless pork loin roast (3 pounds)**
- 1½ **teaspoons salt, divided**
- ¾ **teaspoon pepper, divided**
- ¼ **cup olive oil, divided**
- 3 **medium apples, sliced**
- 1½ **cups unsweetened apple juice**
- 6 **medium onions, sliced (about 5 cups)**
- 3 **tablespoons balsamic vinegar**
- 1½ **cups frozen pitted dark sweet cherries**
- ½ **cup cherry juice**

1. Preheat oven to 350°. Sprinkle roast with 1 teaspoon salt and ½ teaspoon pepper. In an ovenproof Dutch oven, heat 2 tablespoons oil over medium-high heat; brown roast on all sides. Add apples and apple juice to pan. Bake, uncovered, 50-60 minutes or until a thermometer inserted in pork reads 145°, basting occasionally with pan juices.

2. Meanwhile, in a large skillet, heat remaining oil over medium heat. Add onions and remaining salt and pepper; cook and stir 8-10 minutes or until softened. Reduce heat to medium-low; cook 35-40 minutes or until deep golden brown, stirring occasionally. Keep warm.

3. Remove the roast and apples to a serving plate; tent with foil. Let roast stand 10 minutes before slicing.

4. Skim fat from pork pan juices. Place over medium-high heat; add vinegar and cook 1 minute, stirring to loosen browned bits from pan. Stir in cherries and cherry juice. Bring to a boil; cook 10-15 minutes or until mixture is reduced to about 1 cup. Serve pork, apples and onions with the cherry glaze.

1. In a small bowl, mix sour cream, lime peel, cumin and ¼ teaspoon salt. In a large saucepan, heat 1 tablespoon oil over medium heat. Add garlic; cook and stir just until fragrant, about 45 seconds. Stir in beans, pepper sauce, chili powder and remaining salt; heat through, stirring occasionally. Keep warm.

2. Brush both sides of tortillas with remaining oil. Place a large skillet over medium-high heat. Add tortillas in two batches; cook 2-3 minutes on each side or until lightly browned and crisp.

3. To serve, arrange beans and lettuce over tostada shells; top with salsa, sour cream mixture and cheese. Serve with lime wedges.

SATURN'S PIZZA RING

⑤ INGREDIENTS FAST FIX
SATURN'S PIZZA RING

My 7-year-old, Sarah, loves pizza. This is a recipe she came up with, and it was a huge success! You can add any other pizza toppings you like.

—**TRICIA RICHARDSON** SPRINGDALE, AR

START TO FINISH: 30 MIN.
MAKES: 8 SERVINGS

- 1 **pound bulk Italian sausage**
- 1 **can (15 ounces) pizza sauce, divided**
- 1½ **cups shredded part-skim mozzarella cheese, divided**
- 4 **ounces Canadian bacon, chopped**
- 2 **tubes (8 ounces each) refrigerated crescent rolls**

1. Cook sausage in a large skillet over medium heat until no longer pink; drain. Stir in ½ cup pizza sauce, 1 cup cheese and Canadian bacon.
2. Unroll crescent dough and separate into triangles. On an ungreased 14-in. pizza pan, arrange triangles in a ring with points toward the outside and wide ends overlapping at the center, leaving a 4-in. opening. Press overlapping dough to seal.

3. Spoon the filling onto wide end of triangles. Fold pointed end of triangles over filling, tucking points under to form a ring (filling will be visible).
4. Bake at 375° for 12-15 minutes or until golden brown and heated through. Sprinkle with the remaining cheese. Bake 5 minutes longer or until cheese is melted. Serve with remaining pizza sauce.

MY BEST-EVER JAMBALAYA

I tried to mimic jambalaya from my favorite restaurant, and it turned out so well that my daughter and husband now prefer my recipe. They don't order the jambalaya when we go to that restaurant now!

—**ALEXIS VAN VULPEN** ST. ALBERT, AB

PREP: 20 MIN. • **COOK:** 40 MIN.
MAKES: 10 SERVINGS

- 2 **tablespoons canola oil**
- ½ **pound fully cooked Spanish chorizo links, sliced**
- 2 **cups cubed fully cooked ham**
- ¾ **pound boneless skinless chicken breasts, cubed**
- 1 **can (28 ounces) diced tomatoes, undrained**
- 3 **cups chicken broth**
- 2 **large green peppers, chopped**
- 1 **large onion, chopped**
- 1 **tablespoon Cajun seasoning**
- 2 **teaspoons hot pepper sauce**
- 3 **cups instant brown rice**
- ½ **pound uncooked medium shrimp, peeled and deveined**

1. In a Dutch oven, heat the oil over medium-high heat. Add chorizo and ham; cook and stir 3-4 minutes or until browned.
2. Add chicken to pan; cook 5-7 minutes or until no longer pink. Stir in tomatoes, broth, peppers, onion, Cajun seasoning and pepper sauce. Bring to a boil. Reduce heat; simmer, uncovered, 8-10 minutes or until peppers are crisp-tender.
3. Return to a boil; stir in rice and shrimp. Reduce heat; simmer, covered, 7-9 minutes or until shrimp turn pink. Remove from the heat; let stand, covered, 5 minutes or until rice is tender.

CAROLINA SHRIMP & CHEDDAR GRITS

Shrimp and grits are a house favorite, if only we could agree on a recipe! I stirred things up with cheddar and Cajun seasoning to find a true winner.

—**CHARLOTTE PRICE** RALEIGH, NC

PREP: 15 MIN. • **COOK:** 2¾ HOURS
MAKES: 6 SERVINGS

- 1 cup uncooked stone-ground grits
- 1 large garlic clove, minced
- ½ teaspoon salt
- ¼ teaspoon pepper
- 4 cups water
- 2 cups shredded cheddar cheese
- ¼ cup butter, cubed
- 1 pound peeled and deveined cooked shrimp (31-40 per pound)
- 2 medium tomatoes, seeded and finely chopped
- 4 green onions, finely chopped
- 2 tablespoons chopped fresh parsley
- 4 teaspoons lemon juice
- 2 to 3 teaspoons Cajun seasoning

1. Place the first five ingredients in a 3-qt. slow cooker; stir to combine. Cook, covered, on high 2½-3 hours or until water is absorbed and grits are tender, stirring every 45 minutes.
2. Stir in cheese and butter until melted. Stir in remaining ingredients; cook, covered, on high 15-30 minutes or until heated through.

★ ★ ★ ★ ★ **5 STAR TIP**

To cook raw shrimp in water, add 1 pound shrimp (with or without shells, depending on the recipe) and 1 teaspoon salt to 3 quarts boiling water. Reduce heat and simmer, uncovered, for 1-3 minutes or until the shrimp turns pink and curls. Watch closely to avoid overcooking—the meat of uncooked shrimp will turn from translucent when raw to pink and opaque when cooked. Drain immediately.

CAROLINA SHRIMP
& CHEDDAR GRITS

HOMEMADE
POLISH
PIEROGIES

HOMEMADE POLISH PIEROGIES

My mother made many dozens of these over the years and measured ingredients using the palm of her hand. We've passed the recipe down as the family has grown.

—**VERONICA WEINKAUF** SOUTH BEND, IN

PREP: 30 MIN. + STANDING
COOK: 10 MIN./BATCH
MAKES: 8 SERVINGS

- 2 **large eggs**
- ¼ **cup water**
- ½ **teaspoon salt**
- 2 **cups all-purpose flour**

FILLING

- 1 **large egg**
- 1 **teaspoon salt**
- ½ **teaspoon sugar**
  Dash pepper
- 1 **carton (15 to 16 ounces) soft farmer cheese or whole-milk ricotta cheese**
- 1 **to 4 tablespoons butter, divided**
  Sour cream, optional

1. In a large bowl, whisk eggs, water and salt until blended; gradually stir in the flour. Transfer to a lightly floured surface; knead 10-12 times, forming a firm dough. Cover with plastic wrap and let rest 10 minutes.

2. For filling, in a small bowl, whisk egg, salt, sugar and pepper. Stir in cheese.

3. Divide the dough into four portions. On a lightly floured surface, roll each portion to ⅛-in. thickness; cut with a floured 4-in. round cookie cutter. Place 1 tablespoon filling in center of each circle. Moisten edges with water; fold in half and press edges to seal. Repeat with remaining dough and filling.

4. In a 6-qt. stockpot, bring water to a boil. Add the pierogies in batches; reduce the heat to a gentle simmer. Cook 2-3 minutes or until the pierogies float to the top and are tender. Remove with a slotted spoon.

5. In a large skillet, heat 1 tablespoon butter over medium-high heat. Add pierogies in batches; cook 1-3 minutes on each side or until golden brown, adding additional butter as necessary. If desired, serve with sour cream.

BARBECUED STRAWBERRY CHICKEN

BARBECUED STRAWBERRY CHICKEN

When it's time to impress family and friends, we serve barbecued chicken garnished with strawberries. It's easier—and tastier!—than anyone would ever guess.

—**BONNIE HAWKINS** ELKHORN, WI

PREP: 25 MIN. • **BAKE:** 15 MIN.
MAKES: 4 SERVINGS

- 2 **tablespoons canola oil**
- 4 **boneless skinless chicken breast halves (6 ounces each)**
- 2 **tablespoons butter**
- ¼ **cup finely chopped red onion**
- 1 **cup barbecue sauce**
- 2 **tablespoons brown sugar**
- 2 **tablespoons balsamic vinegar**
- 2 **tablespoons honey**
- 1 **cup sliced fresh strawberries**

1. Preheat oven to 350°. In a large ovenproof skillet, heat oil over medium-high heat. Brown the chicken on both sides. Remove from pan. In the same pan, heat the butter over medium-high heat. Add the onion; cook and stir 1 minute or until tender.

2. Stir in barbecue sauce, brown sugar, vinegar and honey. Bring to a boil. Reduce the heat; simmer, uncovered, 4-6 minutes or until thickened. Return chicken to pan. Bake 12-15 minutes or until a thermometer reads 165°. Stir in strawberries.

⑤ INGREDIENTS **FAST FIX**
PERSONAL MARGHERITA PIZZAS

This family-friendly supper is simplicity at its finest. Delectable fresh mozzarella and a sprinkling of basil give these little pies some Italian flair.

—**JERRY GULLEY** PLEASANT PRAIRIE, WI

START TO FINISH: 25 MIN.
MAKES: 3 SERVINGS

- 1 **package (6½ ounces) pizza crust mix**
- ½ **teaspoon dried oregano**
- ¾ **cup pizza sauce**
- 6 **ounces fresh mozzarella cheese, thinly sliced**
- ¼ **cup thinly sliced fresh basil leaves**

1. Preheat oven to 425°. Prepare pizza dough according to package directions, adding oregano before mixing. Divide into three portions.

2. Pat each portion of the dough into an 8-in. circle on greased baking sheets. Bake 8-10 minutes or until edges are lightly browned.

3. Spread each crust with ¼ cup pizza sauce to within ½ in. of edge. Top with cheese. Bake 5-10 minutes longer or until crust is golden and cheese is melted. Sprinkle with basil.

ARTICHOKE & LEMON PASTA

While sailing in the Mediterranean, I tasted a lemony pasta that I fell in love with. I developed my own version of it that our guests now love. Try it with shrimp and kalamata olives, too.

—**PETER HALFERTY** CORPUS CHRISTI, TX

PREP: 20 MIN. • **COOK:** 20 MIN.
MAKES: 6 SERVINGS

- 2½ teaspoons salt, divided
- ½ pound fresh asparagus, trimmed and cut into 1½-inch pieces
- 4 cups uncooked bow tie pasta (about 12 ounces)
- 3 tablespoons olive oil, divided
- 1 can (14 ounces) water-packed quartered artichoke hearts, well drained
- 2 garlic cloves, minced
- 1 cup crumbled goat cheese
- 2 tablespoons minced fresh parsley
- 1 tablespoon grated lemon peel
- 2 to 3 tablespoons lemon juice
- ⅓ cup grated Parmesan cheese

1. Fill a 6-qt. stockpot three-fourths full with water; add 2 teaspoons salt and bring to a boil. Add asparagus; cook, uncovered, 1-2 minutes or just until crisp-tender. Remove asparagus and immediately drop into ice water. Drain and pat dry.

2. In the same pot of water, cook pasta according to package directions for al dente. Drain, reserving 1 cup pasta water. Return pasta to pot.

3. Meanwhile, in a large skillet, heat 1 tablespoon oil over medium-high heat. Add the artichoke hearts; cook and stir 3-4 minutes or until lightly browned. Add garlic; cook 1 minute longer. Add to pasta.

4. Add the asparagus, goat cheese, parsley, lemon peel, lemon juice and remaining salt and oil; toss to combine, adding enough reserved pasta water to coat. Heat through. Serve with the Parmesan cheese.

ARTICHOKE & LEMON PASTA

FAST FIX ▶
BATTER-UP WALLEYE

Nothing is more rewarding than celebrating the day's catch with friends when you share this dish. Substitute your favorite fish if you have something other than walleye.

—**ALESHA OSTER** WILLISTON, ND

START TO FINISH: 30 MIN.
MAKES: 4 SERVINGS

- 1 **cup biscuit/baking mix**
- 1 **tablespoon garlic powder**
- 1 **tablespoon onion powder**
- 1 **tablespoon Cajun seasoning**
- 1½ **teaspoons pepper**
- 1 **teaspoon salt**
- ½ **cup 2% milk**
  Oil for frying
- 1 **pound walleye fillets, skin removed**
  Lemon wedges

1. In a shallow bowl, mix the first six ingredients. Place milk in a separate shallow bowl. In an electric skillet, heat ¼ in. of oil to 375°.

2. In batches, dip the fish in milk, then coat with the baking mix mixture; fry for 5 minutes on each side or until golden brown and fish flakes easily with a fork. Serve immediately with lemon wedges.

BIG JOHN'S CHILI-RUBBED RIBS

When my family thinks of summer grilling, it's ribs all the way. Our Asian-inspired recipe is a welcome change from the usual barbecue-sauce versions.

—**GINGER SULLIVAN** CUTLER BAY, FL

PREP: 20 MIN. + CHILLING
GRILL: 1½ HOURS
MAKES: 10 SERVINGS

- 3 **tablespoons packed brown sugar**
- 2 **tablespoons paprika**
- 2 **tablespoons chili powder**
- 3 **teaspoons ground cumin**
- 2 **teaspoons garlic powder**
- 1 **teaspoon salt**
- 6 **pounds pork baby back ribs**

GLAZE
- 1 **cup reduced-sodium soy sauce**
- 1 **cup packed brown sugar**
- ⅔ **cup ketchup**
- ⅓ **cup lemon juice**
- 1½ **teaspoons minced fresh gingerroot**

1. Mix the first six ingredients; rub over ribs. Refrigerate, covered, 30 minutes.

2. Wrap rib racks in large pieces of heavy-duty foil; seal tightly. Grill, covered, over indirect medium heat 1-1½ hours or until tender.

3. In a large saucepan, combine glaze ingredients; cook, uncovered, over medium heat 6-8 minutes or until heated through and sugar is dissolved, stirring occasionally.

4. Carefully remove ribs from foil. Place ribs over direct heat; brush with some of the glaze. Grill, covered, over medium heat 25-30 minutes or until browned, turning and brushing ribs occasionally with remaining glaze.

⑤ INGREDIENTS
BROWN SUGAR PINEAPPLE HAM

With pineapple, brown sugar, mustard and cloves, this baked ham is straightforward and simple. It's just what you're looking for: a holiday ham with easy steps!

—*TASTE OF HOME* TEST KITCHEN

PREP: 10 MIN. • **BAKE:** 2 HOURS
MAKES: 12 SERVINGS

- 1 **fully cooked bone-in ham (7 to 9 pounds)**
- 1 **can (20 ounces) crushed pineapple, undrained**
- 1 **cup packed brown sugar**
- 1 **tablespoon Dijon mustard**
- ¼ **teaspoon ground cloves**

1. Preheat oven to 325°. Place ham on a rack in a shallow roasting pan. Using a sharp knife, score surface of ham with ½-in.-deep cuts in a diamond pattern. Cover and bake 1½ hours.

2. In a small bowl, mix the remaining ingredients. Spread over the ham, pressing mixture into cuts. Bake ham, uncovered, 30-60 minutes longer or until a thermometer reads 140°.

HOW TO MAKE CROSSHATCH MARKS

*Mmm...*nothing makes mouths start watering at cookouts like those gorgeous crosshatch grill marks on meat. Want to create them on your pork chops? Place the chops on the grill to sear, then rotate them a quarter turn and cook 2-3 minutes longer before flipping to cook on the other side.

ULTIMATE GRILLED PORK CHOPS

A little brining and a special dry rub go a long way to making the perfect pork chop. Once you've mastered the techniques, you'll be enjoying them all summer long.
—**MATTHEW HASS** FRANKLIN, WI

PREP: 20 MIN. + BRINING • **GRILL:** 10 MIN.
MAKES: 4 SERVINGS

- ¼ cup kosher salt
- ¼ cup sugar
- 2 cups water
- 2 cups ice water
- 4 bone-in pork center-cut rib chops (1 inch thick and 8 ounces each)
- 2 tablespoons canola oil

BASIC RUB

- 3 tablespoons paprika
- 1 teaspoon each garlic powder, onion powder, ground cumin and ground mustard
- 1 teaspoon coarsely ground pepper
- ½ teaspoon ground chipotle pepper

1. In a large saucepan, combine salt, sugar and 2 cups water; cook and stir over medium heat until salt and sugar are dissolved. Remove from heat. Add 2 cups ice water to cool the brine to room temperature.

2. Place pork chops in a large resealable plastic bag; add cooled brine. Seal bag, pressing out as much air as possible; turn to coat chops. Place in a 13x9-in. baking dish. Refrigerate 8-12 hours.

3. Remove chops from brine; rinse and pat dry. Discard brine. Brush both sides of chops with oil. In a small bowl, mix rub ingredients; rub over pork chops. Let stand at room temperature 30 minutes. Grill chops on an oiled rack, covered, over medium heat 4-6 minutes on each side or until a thermometer reads 145°. Let stand 5 minutes before serving.

FOR SMOKY PORK RUB *Prepare rub as directed, using smoked paprika in place of regular paprika.*

FOR SPICY PORK RUB *Add ½ teaspoon cayenne pepper to rub mixture.*

FOR SWEET PORK RUB *Add 3 tablespoons brown sugar to rub mixture.*

⑤ INGREDIENTS FAST FIX ▶
ZESTY CHICKEN SOFT TACOS

We've made these tacos with corn and flour tortillas, but flatbread is our favorite wrap. Set out toppings and let everyone assemble his or her own taco.
—**JESSIE GREARSON-SAPAT** FALMOUTH, ME

START TO FINISH: 25 MIN.
MAKES: 6 SERVINGS

- 1 cup (8 ounces) reduced-fat sour cream
- 2 tablespoons Sriracha Asian hot chili sauce
- 2 tablespoons lime juice
- 1½ teaspoons grated lime peel
- ½ teaspoon salt
- ⅛ teaspoon pepper
- 6 naan flatbreads, warmed
- 1 rotisserie chicken, skin removed, shredded
  Minced fresh cilantro, optional

In a small bowl, mix sour cream, chili sauce, lime juice, lime peel, salt and pepper. Spread over flatbreads; top with chicken and, if desired, cilantro.

FAST FIX ▶
PENNE ALLA VODKA

 This easy and impressive pasta is always on the menu when my husband and I invite first-time guests over for dinner. Many friends have asked me to make the recipe again years after they first tried it.
—**CARA LANGER** OVERLAND PARK, KS

START TO FINISH: 30 MIN.
MAKES: 6 SERVINGS

- 1 package (16 ounces) penne pasta
- 3 tablespoons butter
- 2 garlic cloves, minced
- 4 ounces thinly sliced prosciutto, cut into strips
- 1 can (28 ounces) whole plum tomatoes, drained and chopped
- ¼ cup vodka
- ½ teaspoon salt
- ½ teaspoon crushed red pepper flakes
- ½ cup heavy whipping cream
- ½ cup shredded Parmesan cheese

1. Cook pasta according to package directions.

2. Meanwhile, in a large skillet, heat butter over medium-high heat. Add garlic; cook and stir 1 minute. Add prosciutto; cook 2 minutes longer. Stir in tomatoes, vodka, salt and pepper flakes. Bring to a boil. Reduce heat; simmer, uncovered, 5 minutes. Stir in cream; cook 2-3 minutes longer, stirring occasionally.

3. Drain pasta. Add pasta and cheese to sauce; toss to combine.

FAST FIX ▶
PECAN-CRUSTED CHICKEN NUGGETS

I loved chicken nuggets as a child. This baked version is healthier than the original, and it's a great meal for kids.
—**HAILI CARROLL** VALENCIA, CA

START TO FINISH: 30 MIN.
MAKES: 6 SERVINGS

- 1½ cups cornflakes
- 1 tablespoon dried parsley flakes
- 1 teaspoon salt
- ½ teaspoon garlic powder
- ½ teaspoon pepper
- ½ cup panko (Japanese) bread crumbs
- ½ cup finely chopped pecans
- 3 tablespoons 2% milk
- 1½ pounds boneless skinless chicken breasts, cut into 1-inch pieces
  Cooking spray

1. Preheat oven to 400°. Place the cornflakes, parsley, salt, garlic powder and pepper in a blender; cover and pulse until finely ground. Transfer to a shallow bowl; stir in bread crumbs and pecans. Place milk in another shallow bowl. Dip chicken in milk, then roll in crumb mixture to coat.

2. Place on a greased baking sheet; spritz the chicken with cooking spray. Bake 12-16 minutes or until the chicken is no longer pink, turning once halfway through cooking.

RIBEYES WITH HERB BUTTER

The tantalizing fragrance of the herbes de Provence paired with ribeye is unforgettable. The seasoning and herb butter goes well with filet mignon, T-bone and steak strips, too.

—**JOHN BARANSKI** BALDWIN CITY, KS

PREP: 25 MIN. + MARINATING
GRILL: 10 MIN.
MAKES: 4 SERVINGS

- ¼ cup olive oil
- ¼ cup dry red wine
- 1 tablespoon minced fresh rosemary or 1 teaspoon dried rosemary, crushed
- 1 tablespoon red wine vinegar
- 1 tablespoon Dijon mustard
- 1 teaspoon coarsely ground pepper
- 1 teaspoon Worcestershire sauce
- 2 garlic cloves, minced
- 4 beef ribeye steaks (¾ pound each)

STEAK SEASONINGS

- 2 teaspoons kosher salt
- 1 teaspoon sugar
- 1 teaspoon herbes de Provence
- 1 teaspoon coarsely ground pepper

HERB BUTTER

- ¼ cup butter, softened
- 1 tablespoon minced fresh parsley
- 1 teaspoon prepared horseradish

1. In a large resealable plastic bag, combine the first eight ingredients. Add the steaks; seal bag and turn to coat. Refrigerate overnight.

2. Drain and discard the marinade. Combine the steak seasonings; sprinkle over steaks.

3. Grill steaks, covered, over medium heat or broil 3-4 in. from the heat for 5-7 minutes on each side or until meat reaches desired doneness (for medium-rare, a thermometer should read 145°; medium, 160°; well-done, 170°).

4. For herb butter, in a small bowl, beat the butter, parsley and horseradish until blended. Spoon 1 tablespoon herb butter over each steak.

NOTE *Look for herbes de Provence in the spice aisle.*

SPICY ROASTED SAUSAGE, POTATOES AND PEPPERS

SPICY ROASTED SAUSAGE, POTATOES AND PEPPERS

I love to share my cooking, and this hearty meal-in-one has gotten a tasty reputation. People have actually approached me in public to ask for the recipe!

—**LAURIE SLEDGE** BRANDON, MS

PREP: 20 MIN. • **BAKE:** 30 MIN.
MAKES: 4 SERVINGS

- 1 pound potatoes (about 2 medium), peeled and cut into ½-inch cubes
- 1 package (12 ounces) fully cooked andouille chicken sausage links or flavor of your choice, cut into 1-inch pieces
- 1 medium red onion, cut into wedges
- 1 medium sweet red pepper, cut into 1-inch pieces
- 1 medium green pepper, cut into 1-inch pieces
- ½ cup pickled pepper rings
- 1 tablespoon olive oil
- ½ to 1 teaspoon Creole seasoning
- ¼ teaspoon pepper

1. Preheat oven to 400°. In a large bowl, combine the potatoes, sausage, onion, red pepper, green pepper and pepper rings. Mix oil, Creole seasoning and pepper; drizzle over potato mixture and toss to coat.

2. Transfer to a 15x10x1-in. baking pan coated with cooking spray. Roast 30-35 minutes or until vegetables are tender, stirring occasionally.

☆ ☆ ☆ ☆ ☆ **READER REVIEW**

"Laurie's recipe is one of those go-to favorites, very similar to one I make when all else fails. I like the addition of the Creole seasoning to this version."

BEEMA TASTEOFHOME.COM

CANNELLONI-STYLE LASAGNA

I created this lasagna, combining two favorite dishes, for our family's Christmas gathering. It was extra special because my parents had just come back from a trip to Italy.
—**DEBORAH LOOP** CLINTON TOWNSHIP, MI

PREP: 1 HOUR • **BAKE:** 50 MIN. + STANDING
MAKES: 12 SERVINGS

- 1 tablespoon olive oil
- 1 small onion, finely chopped
- ⅓ cup finely chopped celery
- ¼ cup finely chopped carrot
- 2 garlic cloves, minced
- ¾ pound ground beef
- ¾ pound ground pork
- ⅓ cup white wine or beef stock
- ⅔ cup beef stock
- 1 bay leaf
- ¾ teaspoon Italian seasoning
- ½ teaspoon coarsely ground pepper
- ¼ teaspoon salt
- 2 jars (15 ounces each) Alfredo sauce, divided
- 2 large egg yolks
- 1 jar (24 ounces) marinara sauce
- 1 package (9 ounces) no-cook lasagna noodles

1. In a Dutch oven, heat the oil over medium-high heat. Add onion, celery and carrot; cook and stir 4-6 minutes or until tender. Add garlic; cook 1 minute longer.

2. Add beef and pork; cook 4-6 minutes or until meat is no longer pink, breaking into crumbles; drain. Stir in wine. Bring to a boil; cook until the liquid is almost evaporated, about 1 minute.

3. Stir in the stock and seasonings; bring to a boil. Reduce heat; simmer, covered, 15 minutes to allow flavors to blend. Cool slightly. Remove bay leaf; stir in 1 cup Alfredo sauce and egg yolks.

4. Preheat oven to 350°. To assemble, spread ¾ cup marinara sauce into a greased 13x9-in. baking dish. Layer dish with four noodles, ¾ cup Alfredo sauce and 2 cups meat mixture. Top with four noodles and ¾ cup marinara sauce. Layer with four noodles, ¾ cup Alfredo sauce and remaining meat mixture. Top with remaining noodles and marinara sauce. Drizzle remaining Alfredo sauce over top.

5. Bake, covered, 30 minutes. Uncover; bake 20-25 minutes longer or until bubbly. Let stand 15 minutes before serving.

TURKEY CLUB ROULADES

Weeknights turn elegant when these short-prep roulades with familiar ingredients are on the menu. Not a fan of turkey? Substitute lightly pounded chicken breasts.
—*TASTE OF HOME* TEST KITCHEN

PREP: 20 MIN. • **COOK:** 15 MIN.
MAKES: 8 SERVINGS

- ¾ pound fresh asparagus, trimmed
- 8 turkey breast cutlets (about 1 pound)
- 1 tablespoon Dijon-mayonnaise blend
- 8 slices deli ham
- 8 slices provolone cheese
- ½ teaspoon poultry seasoning
- ½ teaspoon pepper
- 8 bacon strips

SAUCE

- ⅔ cup Dijon-mayonnaise blend
- 4 teaspoons 2% milk
- ¼ teaspoon poultry seasoning

1. Bring 4 cups water to a boil in a large saucepan. Add the asparagus; cook, uncovered, for 3 minutes or until crisp-tender. Drain and immediately place asparagus in ice water. Drain and pat dry. Set aside.

2. Spread the turkey cutlets with Dijon-mayonnaise. Layer with ham, cheese and asparagus. Sprinkle with poultry seasoning and pepper. Roll up tightly and wrap with bacon.

3. Cook roulades in a large skillet over medium-high heat for 12-15 minutes, turning occasionally, or until bacon is crisp and turkey is no longer pink. Combine the sauce ingredients; serve with roulades.

★ ★ ★ ★ ★ **5 STAR TIP**

In order to keep asparagus fresh longer, I place the cut stems in a container of cold water—similar to flowers in a vase. I keep the asparagus in the refrigerator, changing the water at least once every three days.
—**MARY S.** COUNCIL BLUFFS, IA

CANNELLONI-STYLE LASAGNA

FRENCH ONION PIZZA AU GRATIN

I love a hot bowl of French onion soup and am also a big fan of pizza. I combined the two classics into an unforgettable dinner!
—**BONNIE LONG** LAKEWOOD, OH

PREP: 30 MIN. • **BAKE:** 10 MIN.
MAKES: 8 SLICES

- 1 large onion, sliced
- 2 tablespoons brown sugar
- 2 tablespoons olive oil, divided
- 3 tablespoons balsamic vinegar
- 3 garlic cloves, minced
- 1 tablespoon bourbon, optional
- 1 cup sliced fresh mushrooms
- ¼ pound thickly sliced deli roast beef, coarsely chopped
- 1 prebaked 12-inch pizza crust
- ¾ cup French onion dip
- ¾ cup shredded part-skim mozzarella cheese
- 1 medium sweet red pepper, chopped
- ¾ cup shredded Gruyere or Swiss cheese
- 1 teaspoon minced fresh rosemary

1. In a large skillet, saute the onion with brown sugar in 1 tablespoon oil until softened. Reduce the heat to medium-low; cook, stirring occasionally, for 30 minutes or until deep golden brown. Stir in vinegar and garlic. Remove from heat; add bourbon if desired. Continue cooking until liquid is nearly evaporated.
2. In another skillet, saute mushrooms in remaining oil until tender; add roast beef and heat through.
3. Place crust on a pizza pan; spread with French onion dip. Layer with mozzarella cheese, the onion mixture, red pepper, mushroom mixture and Gruyere cheese.
4. Bake at 425° for 10-15 minutes or until cheese is melted. Sprinkle with rosemary.

FRENCH ONION PIZZA AU GRATIN

GRILLED PINEAPPLE PORK & VEGETABLES

Celebrate the weekend with a tasty grilled dinner. The pork takes just an hour to marinate, so you'll enjoy a little hands-free time with this carefree meal.

—*TASTE OF HOME* TEST KITCHEN

PREP: 25 MIN. + MARINATING
GRILL: 15 MIN.
MAKES: 5 SERVINGS

- 1 can (8 ounces) unsweetened pineapple chunks, undrained
- ¼ cup olive oil, divided
- 2 garlic cloves, peeled and halved
- 2 teaspoons ground cumin
- 2 teaspoons dried oregano
- ¾ teaspoon pepper, divided
- ¾ teaspoon salt, divided
- 2 pounds pork tenderloin, cut into ¾-inch slices
- 1 pound fresh asparagus, trimmed
- 4 medium carrots, halved lengthwise
- 1 large sweet red pepper, halved
- 1 bunch green onions, trimmed

1. Place the pineapple, 2 tablespoons oil, garlic, cumin, oregano, ½ teaspoon pepper and ¼ teaspoon salt in a blender; cover and process until blended. Place in a large resealable plastic bag; add the pork. Seal the bag and turn to coat; refrigerate 1 hour.

2. Drain and discard the marinade. Place pork on greased grill rack. Grill, uncovered, over medium heat for 3-4 minutes on each side or until a thermometer reads 145°. Let stand for 5 minutes before serving.

3. Place vegetables in a grill wok or basket. Brush with the remaining oil; sprinkle with remaining salt and pepper.

4. Grill, uncovered, over medium heat for 6-8 minutes or until tender, stirring frequently. Cut vegetables into 2-in. pieces. Serve with pork.

NOTE *If you do not have a grill wok or basket, use a disposable foil pan. Poke holes in the bottom of the pan with a meat fork to allow liquid to drain.*

FONTINA ROLLED CHICKEN

FONTINA ROLLED CHICKEN

Good food has a way of transporting you to faraway places. My chicken dish with fontina and cream cheese is like a blissful trip overseas.

—**TAMMY REX** NEW TRIPOLI, PA

PREP: 30 MIN. • **BAKE:** 30 MIN.
MAKES: 4 SERVINGS

- 4 ounces cream cheese, softened
- 1 cup shredded fontina cheese
- 5 bacon strips, cooked and crumbled
- 4 green onions, chopped
- ¼ cup chopped fresh Italian parsley
- ¼ cup julienned oil-packed sun-dried tomatoes, drained, chopped and patted dry
- ½ teaspoon salt, divided
- ¾ teaspoon pepper, divided
- 1 large egg
- 1½ cups panko (Japanese) bread crumbs
- 1 teaspoon paprika
- 4 boneless skinless chicken breast halves (6 ounces each)
- 1 tablespoon olive oil

1. Preheat oven to 375°. In a bowl, mix first six ingredients; stir in ¼ teaspoon each salt and pepper. In a shallow bowl, whisk egg and the remaining salt and pepper. In another shallow bowl, toss bread crumbs with paprika.

2. Carefully pound chicken breasts with a meat mallet to ¼-in. thickness. Spread cheese mixture over chicken. Roll up chicken from a short side; secure with toothpicks.

3. Dip chicken in egg, then coat with crumbs. Place in a foil-lined 15x10x1-in. baking pan, seam side down. Drizzle tops with oil.

4. Bake, uncovered, 30-35 minutes or until golden brown and chicken is no longer pink. Let stand 5 minutes; discard toothpicks before serving.

JUST PEACHY PORK TENDERLOIN

ANDOUILLE-STUFFED PEPPERS

I was inspired by the important role of green peppers in Cajun dishes when I created my spiced-up recipe. For a healthy choice, substitute chicken sausage or cubed cooked chicken breast for the andouille.

—**SARAH LARSON** CARLSBAD, CA

PREP: 40 MIN. • **BAKE:** 40 MIN.
MAKES: 4 SERVINGS

- 1 **package (8 ounces) jambalaya mix**
- 4 **small green peppers**
- ¾ **pound fully cooked andouille sausage links, chopped**
- 1 **jalapeno pepper, seeded and minced**
- 1 **can (16 ounces) tomato juice Louisiana-style hot sauce, optional**

1. Prepare jambalaya mix according to package directions. Meanwhile, cut peppers lengthwise in half; remove seeds.
2. In a large skillet, cook and stir sausage over medium-high heat until browned. Add jalapeno; cook 1 minute longer.
3. Stir sausage mixture into prepared jambalaya. Spoon into pepper halves. Place in a greased 13x9-in. baking dish; pour tomato juice over and around peppers.
4. Bake, uncovered, at 350° for 40-45 minutes or until peppers are tender. Serve with hot sauce if desired.
NOTES *This recipe was prepared with Zatarain's New Orleans-style Jambalaya mix. Wear disposable gloves when cutting hot peppers; the oils can burn skin. Avoid touching your face.*

★ ★ ★ ★ ★ **5 STAR TIP**
Want to make stuffed peppers but don't have any rice on hand? Don't worry! Try cooked barley or whole kernel corn in place of the rice. Adding a tablespoon or two of quick-cooking oats helps to keep the dishes from getting too saucy after baking.

JUST PEACHY PORK TENDERLOIN

I had a pork tenderloin and ripe peaches and decided to put them together. The results couldn't have been more irresistible! Enjoy a fresh entree that tastes like summer.

—**JULIA GOSLIGA** ADDISON, VT

START TO FINISH: 20 MIN.
MAKES: 4 SERVINGS

- 1 **pound pork tenderloin, cut into 12 slices**
- ½ **teaspoon salt**
- ¼ **teaspoon pepper**
- 2 **teaspoons olive oil**
- 4 **medium peaches, peeled and sliced**
- 1 **tablespoon lemon juice**
- ¼ **cup peach preserves**

1. Flatten each tenderloin slice to ¼-in. thickness. Sprinkle with salt and pepper. In a large nonstick skillet over medium heat, cook the pork in oil until tender. Remove and keep warm.
2. Add peaches and lemon juice, stirring to loosen browned bits from pan. Cook and stir for 3-4 minutes or until peaches are tender. Stir in the pork and preserves; heat through.

SOUTHWEST KIELBASA BOWLS

Here's our at-home take on restaurant burrito bowls. We start with rice, kielbasa and black beans, then top 'em with salsa, red onion and cilantro. Use a spicier sausage if you want to crank up the heat.

—**ABBY WILLIAMSON** DUNEDIN, FL

START TO FINISH: 20 MIN.
MAKES: 4 SERVINGS

- 2 **cups uncooked instant brown rice**
- 2 **tablespoons olive oil**
- 1 **package (14 ounces) smoked turkey kielbasa, cut into ¼-inch slices**
- 1 **can (15 ounces) black beans, rinsed and drained**
- 1½ **cups fresh salsa**
- ¼ **cup finely chopped red onion Fresh cilantro leaves, optional**

1. Cook rice according to package directions.
2. Meanwhile, in a large skillet, heat oil over medium-high heat. Add kielbasa; cook and stir 4-6 minutes or until browned. Stir in beans and salsa. Divide rice among four bowls. Top with kielbasa mixture, onion and, if desired, cilantro.

"Who would have thought to put strawberries and salmon together?! It works and is quite delicious and fresh tasting. I may try broiling the salmon next time."

FAST FIX

SEARED SALMON WITH STRAWBERRY BASIL RELISH

Take a sweet new approach to salmon by topping it off with a relish of strawberries, basil, honey and pepper.

—**STACY MULLENS** GRESHAM, OR

START TO FINISH: 20 MIN.
MAKES: 6 SERVINGS

- 6 salmon fillets (4 ounces each)
- 1 tablespoon butter, melted
- ¼ teaspoon salt
- ⅛ teaspoon freshly ground pepper

RELISH
- 1¼ cups finely chopped fresh strawberries
- 1 tablespoon minced fresh basil
- 1 tablespoon honey
  Dash freshly ground pepper

1. Brush fillets with melted butter; sprinkle with salt and pepper. Heat a large skillet over medium-high heat. Add the fillets, skin side up, in batches if necessary; cook 2-3 minutes on each side or until fish just begins to flake easily with a fork.

2. In a small bowl, toss strawberries with basil, honey and pepper. Serve salmon with relish.

ANDOUILLE-STUFFED PEPPERS

SEARED SALMON WITH STRAWBERRY BASIL RELISH

BREADS
& ROLLS

★★★★★

Nothing transforms a house into a home faster than the aroma of fresh-baked bread. Create your own down-home atmosphere with these tried-and-true recipes!

HONEY WHOLE WHEAT ROLLS

Most of the farmers in our area grow wheat, so this recipe definitely represents my region. I bake these rolls often, especially when I'm making soup or stew.

—**CELECIA STOUP** HOBART, OK

PREP: 20 MIN. + RISING • **BAKE:** 20 MIN.
MAKES: 15 ROLLS

- 2 **packages (¼ ounce each) active dry yeast**
- 1 **cup warm water (110° to 115°)**
- ¼ **cup butter, melted**
- ¼ **cup honey**
- 1 **large egg**
- ¾ **cup whole wheat flour**
- ½ **cup old-fashioned oats**
- 1 **teaspoon salt**
- 2¼ **to 2¾ cups all-purpose flour**
  Additional melted butter, optional

1. In a small bowl, dissolve yeast in warm water. In a large bowl, combine butter, honey, egg, whole wheat flour, oats, salt, yeast mixture and 1 cup all-purpose flour; beat on medium until smooth. Stir in enough of the remaining all-purpose flour to form a soft dough.
2. Turn dough onto a floured surface; knead until smooth and elastic, about 6-8 minutes. Place in a greased bowl, turning once to grease the top. Cover with plastic wrap and let rise in a warm place until doubled, about 1 hour.
3. Punch down the dough; shape into 15 balls. Place in a greased 13x9-in. pan. Cover with a kitchen towel; let rise in warm place until doubled, about 45 minutes. Preheat oven to 375°.
4. Bake until golden brown, about 20 minutes. If desired, brush with additional butter. Serve warm.

★ ★ ★ ★ ★ **READER REVIEW**

"What delicious rolls! They were not difficult to make for this first-time wheat bread baker. This recipe is one I will use again and again."

EVELYNDEVRIES TASTEOFHOME.COM

MONKEY BREAD BISCUITS

AUSTRIAN APPLE TWISTS

The addition of apples makes these sweet butterhorns stand out. The recipe is a cinch to prepare because you don't have to wait for the dough to rise.

—**KATHY BLESS** FAYETTEVILLE, PA

PREP: 30 MIN. + CHILLING • **BAKE:** 20 MIN.
MAKES: 64 TWISTS

- 1 package (¼ ounce) active dry yeast
- 3 cups all-purpose flour
- 1 cup butter, softened
- 3 large egg yolks, beaten
- 1 cup (8 ounces) sour cream
- ½ cup sugar
- ½ cup finely chopped pecans
- ¾ teaspoon ground cinnamon
- 1 medium tart apple, peeled and finely chopped

ICING

- 1 cup confectioners' sugar
- 4 teaspoons milk
- ¼ teaspoon vanilla extract
  Finely chopped pecans

1. In a large bowl, combine yeast and flour; add butter and mix well. Add egg yolks and sour cream; mix well. Shape into four balls. Place in separate resealable plastic bags or wrap in plastic wrap; refrigerate overnight.

2. Combine the sugar, pecans and cinnamon; set aside. On a floured surface, roll each ball of dough into a 9-in. circle. Sprinkle with the sugar mixture and apple. Cut each circle into 16 wedges; roll up from the wide edge and pinch to seal. Place with point side down on greased baking sheets.

3. Bake at 350° for 16-20 minutes or until lightly browned. Immediately remove to wire racks to cool. For icing, combine sugar, milk and vanilla until smooth; drizzle over the twists. Sprinkle with pecans.

NOTE *The yeast does not need to be dissolved in liquid, and no rising time is necessary before baking.*

---

(5) INGREDIENTS FAST FIX

MONKEY BREAD BISCUITS

Classic monkey bread usually is a sweetly spiced breakfast treat. I came up with an easy dinner version featuring garlic and Italian seasoning the crowd will love.

—**DANA JOHNSON** SCOTTSDALE, AZ

START TO FINISH: 20 MIN.
MAKES: 1 DOZEN

- 1 tube (16.3 ounces) large refrigerated flaky biscuits
- 3 tablespoons butter, melted
- 1 garlic clove, minced
- ½ teaspoon Italian seasoning
- ¼ cup grated Parmesan cheese
  Additional Italian seasoning

1. Preheat oven to 425°. Separate biscuits; cut each into six pieces. In a large bowl, combine butter, garlic and Italian seasoning; add biscuit pieces and toss to coat.

2. Place four pieces in each of 12 greased muffin cups. Sprinkle with cheese and additional Italian seasoning. Bake for 8-10 minutes or until golden brown. Serve warm.

---

(5) INGREDIENTS FAST FIX

SUN-DRIED TOMATO GARLIC BREAD

My fast bread recipe comes together in minutes. It tastes terrific with a variety of main courses, is easy enough for a weekday, but special enough for a meal with guests.

—**NADINE MESCH** MOUNT HEALTHY, OH

START TO FINISH: 10 MIN.
MAKES: 6 SERVINGS

- ¼ cup butter, softened
- ¼ cup grated Parmesan cheese
- 2 tablespoons chopped oil-packed sun-dried tomatoes
- 1 to 2 garlic cloves, minced
- ½ loaf Italian bread, halved lengthwise

1. In a small bowl, combine butter, cheese, tomatoes and garlic. Spread over the cut sides of bread. Transfer to an ungreased baking sheet.

2. Broil 4 in. from the heat 3-4 minutes or until golden brown. Cut into slices and serve warm.

AUSTRIAN APPLE TWISTS

ORANGE CRANBERRY BREAD

The beauty of this festive quick bread is that it makes a delicious post-dinner snack as well as breakfast the next day. I like to toast leftover slices and spread them with cream cheese or butter for breakfast.

—RON GARDNER GRAND HAVEN, MI

PREP: 20 MIN. • **BAKE:** 50 MIN. + COOLING
MAKES: 2 LOAVES (16 SLICES EACH)

- 2¾ cups all-purpose flour
- ⅔ cup sugar
- ⅔ cup packed brown sugar
- 3½ teaspoons baking powder
- 1 teaspoon salt
- ½ teaspoon ground cinnamon
- ¼ teaspoon ground nutmeg
- 1 large egg
- 1 cup 2% milk
- ½ cup orange juice
- 3 tablespoons canola oil
- 2 to 3 teaspoons grated orange peel
- 2 cups coarsely chopped fresh or frozen cranberries
- 1 large apple, peeled and chopped

1. In a large bowl, combine the flour, sugars, baking powder, salt, cinnamon and nutmeg. Whisk the egg, milk, orange juice, oil and orange peel; stir into the dry ingredients just until blended. Fold in the cranberries and apple.

2. Pour into two greased 8x4-in. loaf pans. Bake at 350° for 50-55 minutes or until a toothpick inserted near the center comes out clean. Cool for 10 minutes before removing from pans to wire racks.

FREEZE OPTION *Securely wrap cooled loaves in plastic wrap and foil and freeze. To use, thaw at room temperature.*

★ ★ ★ ★ ★ 5 STAR TIP

Substituting whole wheat flour for all-purpose flour is a great way to sneak extra fiber into your diet. For best results, use equal proportions of whole wheat flour and all-purpose flour. Keep in mind that baked goods made with whole wheat flour tend to be denser and have a coarser texture.

ORANGE CRANBERRY BREAD

APPLE & CHEDDAR MINI SCONES

Cheese and sage go well with apples, so why not with scones? These mini scones add zip to a party, brunch or tailgate.

—**SUE GRONHOLZ** BEAVER DAM, WI

PREP: 25 MIN. • **BAKE:** 10 MIN.
MAKES: 32 SCONES

- 3 **cups all-purpose flour**
- 3 **teaspoons baking powder**
- ½ **teaspoon salt**
- ½ **teaspoon baking soda**
- 1 **cup cold butter**
- 1 **large egg**
- ¾ **cup (6 ounces) vanilla yogurt**
- 3 **tablespoons 2% milk, divided**
- ⅓ **cup shredded peeled apple**
- ⅓ **cup shredded sharp cheddar cheese**
- 1 **tablespoon minced fresh sage**
- 1 **tablespoon sugar**

1. Preheat oven to 425°. In a large bowl, whisk flour, baking powder, salt and baking soda. Cut in butter until the mixture resembles coarse crumbs. In another bowl, whisk egg, yogurt and 2 tablespoons milk; stir into the crumb mixture just until moistened. Stir in apple, cheese and sage.

2. Turn onto a lightly floured surface; knead gently 10 times. Divide the dough in half; pat each portion into a 6-in. circle. Cut each circle into eight wedges; cut each wedge in half.

3. Transfer to parchment paper-lined baking sheets. Brush tops with the remaining milk; sprinkle with sugar. Bake 10-12 minutes or until golden brown. Serve warm.

FOR REGULAR-SIZE SCONES *Do not cut wedges in half. Bake as directed, increasing baking time to 12-14 minutes. Makes: 16 regular scones*

APPLE & CHEDDAR MINI SCONES

CHOCOLATE BISCUIT PUFFS

I dreamed up my favorite snack at age 9, so I know kids love to make puffs that hide a chocolate surprise inside.

—**JOY CLARK** SEABECK, WA

START TO FINISH: 20 MIN.
MAKES: 10 SERVINGS

- 1 tube (12 ounces) refrigerated buttermilk biscuits
- 1 milk chocolate candy bar (1.55 ounces)
- 2 teaspoons cinnamon-sugar

1. Preheat oven to 450°. Flatten each biscuit into a 3-in. circle. Break candy bar into 10 pieces; place a piece of candy on each biscuit. Bring up edges to enclose candy and pinch to seal.
2. Place seam side down on an ungreased baking sheet. Sprinkle with cinnamon-sugar. Bake 8-10 minutes or until golden brown.

PUMPKIN CHOCOLATE LOAF

These decadent chocolate loaves, with a hint of pumpkin and spice, have been a favorite of mine for years. They can be sliced to serve as snacks or dessert.

—**KATHY GARDNER** ROCKVILLE, MD

PREP: 15 MIN.
BAKE: 55 MIN. + COOLING + FREEZING
MAKES: 3 LOAVES

- 3¾ cups all-purpose flour
- 3½ cups sugar
- 1½ teaspoons salt
- 1½ teaspoons baking powder
- 1¼ teaspoons baking soda
- 1¼ teaspoons ground cinnamon
- 1 to 1¼ teaspoons ground cloves
- ½ teaspoon ground nutmeg
- 3 large eggs
- 1 can (29 ounces) solid-pack pumpkin
- 1¼ cups canola oil
- 3 ounces unsweetened chocolate, melted and cooled
- 1½ teaspoons vanilla extract
- 2 cups (12 ounces) semisweet chocolate chips

1. In a large bowl, combine flour, sugar, salt, baking powder, baking soda, cinnamon, cloves and nutmeg. In another large bowl, whisk eggs, pumpkin, oil, chocolate and vanilla. Stir into the dry ingredients just until moistened. Fold in chips.
2. Transfer to three greased 9x5-in. loaf pans. Bake at 350° for 55-65 minutes or until a toothpick inserted near the center comes out clean. Cool for 10 minutes before removing from pans to wire racks. Wrap and freeze for up to 6 months.

RICOTTA-RAISIN COFFEE CAKE

A few ingredients come together quickly so I can have a warm coffee cake to serve overnight guests for breakfast. If you don't have or don't like cardamom, substitute any sweet spice. I recommend ground nutmeg, cinnamon or allspice.

—**CAROL GAUS** ELK GROVE VILLAGE, IL

PREP: 15 MIN. + RISING
BAKE: 20 MIN. + COOLING
MAKES: 12 SERVINGS

- 1 loaf (1 pound) frozen bread dough, thawed
- 1 cup part-skim ricotta cheese
- ¼ cup honey
- ¼ teaspoon ground cardamom
- ¼ teaspoon almond extract
- 1 cup golden raisins
- ¼ cup confectioners' sugar
- 2 to 3 teaspoons fat-free milk

1. On a lightly floured surface, roll dough into a 15x9-in. rectangle. In a small bowl, combine cheese, honey, cardamom and almond extract. Spread filling to within ½ in. of edges. Sprinkle with raisins. Roll up jelly-roll style, starting with a long side; pinch seam to seal. Pinch ends together to form a ring.
2. Place the ring seam side down in a 9-in. round baking pan lined with parchment paper. Cover and let rise until doubled, about 30 minutes.
3. Preheat oven to 350°. With a sharp knife, make 12 shallow slashes in the top of the coffee cake. Bake 20-25 minutes or until golden brown. Cool on a wire rack. In a small bowl, combine confectioners' sugar and milk; drizzle over cake.

GOLDEN CRESCENTS

When my grandchildren take one of these slightly sweet, tender rolls out of the basket, they say, "Grandma, you're the world's best cook." There's no better compliment!

—**BERTHA JOHNSON** INDIANAPOLIS, IN

PREP: 25 MIN. + RISING • **BAKE:** 10 MIN.
MAKES: 2 DOZEN

- 2 packages (¼ ounce each) active dry yeast
- ¾ cup warm water (110° to 115°)
- ½ cup sugar
- 2 large eggs
- ¼ cup butter, softened
- 2 tablespoons shortening
- 1 teaspoon salt
- 4 to 4½ cups all-purpose flour
- 2 tablespoons melted butter plus additional as needed, divided

1. In a large bowl, dissolve yeast in warm water. Add sugar, eggs, softened butter, shortening, salt and 2 cups flour; beat until smooth. Add enough of the remaining flour to form a soft dough. Turn onto a floured surface; knead until smooth and elastic, about 6-8 minutes.
2. Place in a greased bowl, turning once to grease the top. Cover with plastic wrap and let rise in a warm place until doubled, about 1½ hours.
3. Punch dough down; divide in half. Roll each half into a 12-in. circle; brush with 1 tablespoon melted butter; cut into 12 wedges. Roll up wedges from the wide end and place point side down 2 in. apart on greased baking sheets. Curve ends to form crescents. Cover and let rise until doubled, about 45 minutes.
4. Bake at 375° for 8-10 minutes or until golden. Brush with additional melted butter if desired.

★ ★ ★ ★ ★ **5 STAR TIP**

To easily test if rising yeast dough has doubled in size, quickly press two fingers into the dough. If the indentations remain, the dough is ready to be shaped.

—**ANNA JENELL C.** TUTTLE, OK

CHIMICHURRI MONKEY BREAD

CHIMICHURRI MONKEY BREAD

The herby goodness of my favorite sauce shines in this nostalgic bread recipe that comes together quickly, thanks to refrigerated biscuits. Serve warm as an appetizer with marinara for dipping, or as a side to an Italian entree.

—**EDEN DRANGER** LOS ANGELES, CA

PREP: 20 MIN. • **BAKE:** 20 MIN.
MAKES: 12 SERVINGS

- ¼ cup minced fresh parsley
- ¼ cup olive oil
- 2 tablespoons minced fresh oregano
- 1 tablespoon white wine vinegar
- 2 garlic cloves
- ¾ teaspoon kosher salt
- ¼ teaspoon ground cumin
- ¼ teaspoon pepper
- ⅛ teaspoon crushed red pepper flakes
- 2 tubes (12 ounces each) refrigerated buttermilk biscuits

1. In a shallow bowl, combine the first nine ingredients. Cut each biscuit in half and shape into a ball. Roll each ball in the herb mixture.
2. Place biscuit pieces in a greased 10-in. fluted tube pan. Bake at 375° for 18-22 minutes or until golden brown. Cool for 5 minutes before turning out onto a serving plate.

MINI SWISS CHEESE LOAVES

I usually make these tender little loaves in the morning so they're ready to eat at lunchtime. There's nothing better than a sandwich prepared with homemade bread.

—**HELEN WANAMAKER VAIL** GLENSIDE, PA

PREP: 25 MIN. + RISING
BAKE: 25 MIN. + COOLING
MAKES: 4 MINI LOAVES

- 1 package (¼ ounce) active dry yeast
- ½ cup warm water (110° to 115°)
- 1 cup (8 ounces) sour cream
- 2 tablespoons sugar
- 1 teaspoon salt
- ¼ teaspoon baking soda
- 1 large egg
- 2⅓ cups all-purpose flour, divided
- 1 cup (4 ounces) shredded Swiss cheese
- 2 teaspoons sesame seeds

1. In a large bowl, dissolve yeast in warm water. Add sour cream, sugar, salt, baking soda, egg and 1⅓ cups flour. Beat on medium for 3 minutes. Stir in Swiss cheese and remaining flour. Do not knead.
2. Spread the batter into four greased 5x3x2-in. loaf pans. Sprinkle with sesame seeds. Cover and let rise in a warm place until doubled, about 45 minutes.
3. Bake at 350° for 25-30 minutes or until golden brown. Remove from pans to wire racks to cool.

CHOCOLATE CHIP-CRANBERRY SCONES

My daughter started making these as a healthier alternative to cookies, since we seem to like cookies of any kind. Use orange-flavored cranberries if you'd like a more citrusy flavor.

—**NICHOLE JONES** IDAHO FALLS, ID

START TO FINISH: 30 MIN.
MAKES: 1 DOZEN

- 2 **cups all-purpose flour**
- 3 **tablespoons brown sugar**
- 2 **teaspoons baking powder**
- 1 **teaspoon grated orange peel**
- ½ **teaspoon salt**
- ½ **teaspoon baking soda**
- ¼ **cup cold butter**
- 1 **cup (8 ounces) plain yogurt**
- 1 **large egg yolk**
- ½ **cup dried cranberries**
- ½ **cup semisweet chocolate chips**

1. Preheat oven to 400°. In a large bowl, whisk the first six ingredients. Cut in butter until the mixture resembles coarse crumbs. In another bowl, whisk yogurt and egg yolk; stir into crumb mixture just until moistened. Stir in cranberries and chocolate chips.

2. Turn onto a floured surface; knead gently 10 times. Pat dough into an 8-in. circle. Cut into 12 wedges. Place wedges on a baking sheet coated with cooking spray. Bake 10-12 minutes or until golden brown. Serve warm.
FREEZE OPTION *Freeze cooled scones in resealable plastic freezer bags. To use, thaw scones at room temperature or, if desired, microwave each scone on high for 20-30 seconds or until heated through.*

PECAN-RAISIN CINNAMON ROLLS

The tempting aroma of these freshly baked cinnamon rolls always helps them sell fast. I bake hundreds for two annual fundraising events in our community.

—**MARVEL IRVINE** ALTA, CA

PREP: 50 MIN. + RISING
BAKE: 20 MIN./BATCH + COOLING
MAKES: 4 DOZEN

- 11 **to 12 cups all-purpose flour**
- ¾ **cup sugar**
- 3 **packages (¼ ounce each) active dry yeast**
- 3 **teaspoons salt**
- 3½ **cups water**
- 1 **cup canola oil**
- 3 **large eggs**

FILLING
- ¼ **cup butter, melted**
- 1 **cup sugar**
- 3 **teaspoons ground cinnamon**
- 1 **cup chopped pecans**
- 1 **cup raisins**

FROSTING
- ¼ **cup butter, softened**
- 3¾ **cups confectioners' sugar**
- 1 **teaspoon vanilla extract**
- ¼ **teaspoon lemon extract**
- 3 **to 4 tablespoons water**

1. In a very large bowl, combine 8 cups flour, sugar, yeast and salt. In a large saucepan, heat water and oil to 120°-130°. Add to the dry ingredients; beat just until moistened. Add eggs; beat until smooth. Stir in enough of the remaining flour to form a soft dough (dough will be sticky).
2. Turn out onto a floured surface; knead until smooth and elastic, about 6-8 minutes. Cover and let rest for 15 minutes.
3. Turn out onto a lightly floured surface; divide in half. Roll each half into a 24x15-in. rectangle. Brush with butter to within 1/2 in. of edges. Combine sugar and cinnamon; sprinkle over dough. Sprinkle with pecans and raisins.
4. Roll up jelly-roll style, starting with the long sides; pinch seams to seal. Cut each into 24 rolls. Place rolls, cut side up, in four greased 13x9-in. baking pans.
5. Cover and let rise in a warm place until nearly doubled, about 30 minutes. Bake at 425° for 18-22 minutes until golden brown.
6. In a small bowl, combine the butter, confectioners' sugar, extracts and enough water to achieve spreading consistency. Spread over warm rolls. Cool on wire racks.
NOTE *The dough may need to be mixed in two batches, depending on the size of your mixing bowl. To halve the recipe, use 1 package plus 1⅛ teaspoons yeast and 1 egg plus 2 tablespoons beaten egg. The other ingredients can easily be divided in half between batches.*

CHOCOLATE CHIP-CRANBERRY SCONES

SESAME WHEAT BRAIDS

HOW TO BRAID BREADS

- Place three ropes almost touching on a baking sheet. Starting in the middle, loosely bring left rope under center rope. Bring right rope under the new center rope; repeat until you reach the end.

- Turn the pan and repeat braiding, bringing the ropes over instead of under.

- Press each end to seal; tuck ends under.

SESAME WHEAT BRAIDS

When I started making this bread, my husband and our six children liked it so much I was baking every day! I was thrilled when the judges at our county fair gave these braids both a blue ribbon and best of show award!
—**NANCY MONTGOMERY** HARTVILLE, OH

PREP: 30 MIN. + RISING
BAKE: 20 MIN. + COOLING
MAKES: 2 LOAVES (16 SLICES EACH)

- 2 packages (¼ ounce each) active dry yeast
- 2¼ cups warm water (110° to 115°)
- ⅓ cup sugar
- 1 tablespoon canola oil
- 1 cup whole wheat flour
- 2 large eggs
- 1 tablespoon water
- 1 tablespoon salt
- 5 to 6 cups all-purpose flour
- 2 teaspoons sesame seeds

1. In a large bowl, dissolve yeast in water. Add sugar and oil; mix well. Stir in whole wheat flour; let stand until the mixture bubbles, about 5 minutes.
2. In a small bowl, beat eggs and water. Remove 2 tablespoons to a small bowl; cover and refrigerate. Add the remaining egg mixture and salt to the batter; mix until smooth. Add 4 cups all-purpose flour and beat until smooth. Add enough remaining flour to form a soft dough.
3. Turn out dough onto a floured surface; knead until smooth and elastic, about 6-8 minutes. Place in a greased bowl, turning once to grease top. Cover and let rise in a warm place until doubled, about 1 hour. Punch dough down and divide in half. Divide each half into thirds.
4. Shape each piece into a rope about 15 in. long. Place three ropes on a greased baking sheet; braid. Pinch each end firmly and tuck under.
5. Brush with the reserved egg mixture; sprinkle with sesame seeds. Repeat, placing the second braid on the same baking sheet. Let rise until doubled, about 45 minutes. Bake at 350° for 20-25 minutes. Remove from the baking sheet to cool on a wire rack.

BANANA MOCHA-CHIP MUFFINS

These moist muffins combine my two favorite things: chocolate and coffee. The banana is just an added bonus!

—**MELISSA WILLIAMS** TAYLORVILLE, IL

PREP: 20 MIN. • **BAKE:** 20 MIN.
MAKES: 2 DOZEN

- 5 teaspoons instant coffee granules
- 5 teaspoons hot water
- ¾ cup butter, softened
- 1¼ cups sugar
- 1 large egg
- 1⅓ cups mashed ripe bananas
- 1 teaspoon vanilla extract
- 2¼ cups all-purpose flour
- 1½ teaspoons baking powder
- ½ teaspoon baking soda
- ½ teaspoon salt
- 1½ cups semisweet chocolate chips

1. Preheat oven to 350°. In a small bowl, dissolve the coffee granules in hot water. In a large bowl, cream butter and sugar until light and fluffy. Add egg; beat well. Beat in the bananas, vanilla and coffee mixture. Combine flour, baking powder, baking soda and salt; add to the creamed mixture just until moistened. Fold in the chocolate chips.

2. Fill paper-lined muffin cups two-thirds full. Bake 18-20 minutes or until a toothpick inserted in muffin comes out clean. Cool 5 minutes before removing from pans to wire racks. Serve warm.

★ ★ ★ ★ ★ **READER REVIEW**

"Boy, were these good! The only thing I did different was use mini chocolate chips. They are very moist and addicting! Bet you can't eat just one!"

TWINS1111 TASTEOFHOME.COM

FREEZE IT
BUTTONS AND BOWS

Biscuit mix hurries along these nutmeg-spiced buttons and bows. This recipe remains a Saturday morning favorite at our house. Serve the sugar-coated treats with hot coffee for dunking.

—**MARCIE HOLLADAY** IRVING, TX

PREP: 20 MIN. • **BAKE:** 10 MIN.
MAKES: 1 DOZEN BUTTONS AND BOWS

- 2 cups biscuit/baking mix
- 2 tablespoons plus ¼ cup sugar, divided
- 1 teaspoon ground nutmeg
- ⅛ teaspoon ground cinnamon
- 1 large egg, beaten
- ⅓ cup 2% milk
- ¼ cup butter, melted

1. In a large bowl, combine biscuit mix, 2 tablespoons sugar, nutmeg and cinnamon. Combine egg and milk; stir into dry ingredients just until moistened.

2. Turn onto a heavily floured surface; knead 5-6 times. Roll out to ¼-in. thickness. Cut with a floured 2½-in. doughnut cutter; set centers aside for buttons.

3. For bows, twist each circle to form a figure eight; place on a greased baking sheet. Bake at 400° for 8-10 minutes or until golden brown. Place buttons on another greased baking sheet. Bake for 6-7 minutes.

4. Brush tops of buttons and bows with butter; sprinkle with the remaining sugar. Remove from pans to wire racks. Serve warm.

FREEZE OPTION *Freeze cooled biscuits in resealable plastic freezer bags, putting the bows in one bag and the buttons in another. To use, place bows on one baking sheet and buttons on another. Heat in a preheated 350° oven 6-8 minutes for bows and 2-4 minutes for buttons or until heated through.*

BUTTONS AND BOWS

DESSERTS
★ ★ ★ ★ ★

When it's time to bring out the finale to your meal, serve a stunner! Whether you're craving cookies, cake, bars or something else, we've rounded up the most decadent desserts for you.

TOFFEE BROWNIE TRIFLE

Dress up a brownie mix in a whole new way! Try this trifle with other flavors of pudding or substitute your favorite candy bar. If you prefer, it also tastes great with low-fat and sugar-free products.
—**WENDY BENNETT** SIOUX FALLS, SD

PREP: 20 MIN. • **BAKE:** 25 MIN. + COOLING
MAKES: 16 SERVINGS

- 1 **package fudge brownie mix (13x9-inch pan size)**
- 2½ **cups cold milk**
- 1 **package (3.4 ounces) instant cheesecake or vanilla pudding mix**
- 1 **package (3.3 ounces) instant white chocolate pudding mix**
- 1 **carton (8 ounces) frozen whipped topping, thawed**
- 2 **to 3 Heath candy bars (1.4 ounces each), chopped**

1. Prepare and bake brownies according to the package directions for cake-like brownies, using a greased 13x9-in. baking pan. Cool completely on a wire rack.
2. In a large bowl, beat milk and pudding mixes on low speed for 2 minutes. Let stand for 2 minutes or until soft-set. Fold in whipped topping.
3. Cut brownies into 1-in. cubes; place half in a 3-qt. glass trifle bowl or serving dish. Cover with half of the pudding. Repeat layers. Sprinkle with chopped candy bars. Refrigerate leftovers.

☆ ☆ ☆ ☆ ☆ **READER REVIEW**
"I made this for a baby shower and it was a huge hit! I put chocolate chunks in the brownies, layered toffee bits on both pudding layers and lined the top with Hershey's kisses. Divine!"
TMYERS TASTEOFHOME.COM

BLUEBERRY ZUCCHINI SQUARES

I saw a bar recipe using apple and lemon peel on a muffin mix box. I tried it from scratch with shredded zucchini and fresh blueberries instead. It's a winner!

—SHELLY BEVINGTON HERMISTON, OR

PREP: 30 MIN. • **BAKE:** 30 MIN. + COOLING
MAKES: 2 DOZEN

- **2 cups shredded zucchini (do not pack)**
- **½ cup buttermilk**
- **1 tablespoon grated lemon peel**
- **3 tablespoons lemon juice**
- **1 cup butter, softened**
- **2½ cups sugar**
- **2 large eggs**
- **3¼ cups plus 2 tablespoons all-purpose flour, divided**
- **1 teaspoon baking soda**
- **½ teaspoon salt**
- **2 cups fresh or frozen blueberries**

GLAZE

- **2 cups confectioners' sugar**
- **¼ cup buttermilk**
- **1 tablespoon grated lemon peel**
- **2 teaspoons lemon juice**
- **⅛ teaspoon salt**

1. Preheat oven to 350°. Grease a 15x10x1-in. baking pan.

2. In a small bowl, combine zucchini, buttermilk, lemon peel and lemon juice; toss to combine. In a large bowl, cream butter and sugar until light and fluffy. Beat in eggs, one at a time. In another bowl, whisk 3¼ cups flour, baking soda and salt; gradually add to the creamed mixture alternately with the zucchini mixture, mixing well after each addition. Toss blueberries with remaining flour; fold into batter.

3. Transfer batter to prepared pan, spreading evenly (pan will be full). Bake 30-35 minutes or until light golden brown and a toothpick inserted in center comes out clean. Cool completely in pan on a wire rack.

4. In a small bowl, mix glaze ingredients until smooth; spread over top. Let stand until set.

NOTE *If using frozen blueberries, use without thawing to avoid discoloring the batter.*

PINEAPPLE UPSIDE-DOWN CHEESECAKE

My mom often made pineapple upside-down cake, but I prefer something creamier. This recipe looks just like her cake, but gets even tastier and more decadent as pineapple upside-down cheesecake.

—MARILYN MCGINNIS CITRUS HEIGHTS, CA

PREP: 25 MIN. • **BAKE:** 35 MIN. + CHILLING
MAKES: 4 SERVINGS

- **¾ cup packed brown sugar**
- **4 slices canned pineapple**
- **4 maraschino cherries**

FILLING

- **1 package (8 ounces) cream cheese, softened**
- **½ cup confectioners' sugar**
- **2 teaspoons all-purpose flour**
- **1 teaspoon vanilla extract**
- **1 large egg, lightly beaten**
- **¼ cup crushed pineapple, well drained**

CRUST

- **1 tablespoon butter**
- **⅓ cup graham cracker crumbs**
- **¼ teaspoon ground cinnamon**

1. Preheat oven to 325°. Sprinkle brown sugar into an 8-in. ovenproof skillet. Arrange pineapple in a single layer over brown sugar; place a cherry in the center of each pineapple slice.

2. For filling, in a large bowl, beat cream cheese and confectioners' sugar until smooth. Beat in flour and vanilla. Add egg; beat on low speed just until blended. Fold in crushed pineapple. Spoon over the fruit.

3. Bake 35-40 minutes or until the center is almost set. Cool on a wire rack 10 minutes. Loosen sides from pan with a knife. Cool 1 hour longer. Refrigerate overnight, covering when cheesecake is completely cooled.

4. For crust, in a small skillet, melt butter over medium-low heat. Add cracker crumbs and cinnamon; cook and stir 4-6 minutes or until toasted. Cool. Just before serving, top cheesecake with toasted crumbs, pressing to adhere. Invert cheesecake onto a serving plate.

CHOCOLATE CHIFFON CAKE

If you want to offer a dessert that really stands out from the rest, this is the cake. Beautiful high layers of rich sponge cake are drizzled with a succulent chocolate glaze.

—ERMA FOX MEMPHIS, MO

PREP: 25 MIN. + COOLING
BAKE: 1 HOUR + COOLING
MAKES: 16-20 SERVINGS

- **7 large eggs, separated**
- **½ cup baking cocoa**
- **¾ cup boiling water**
- **1¾ cups cake flour**
- **1¾ cups sugar**
- **1½ teaspoons baking soda**
- **1 teaspoon salt**
- **½ cup canola oil**
- **2 teaspoons vanilla extract**
- **¼ teaspoon cream of tartar**

ICING

- **⅓ cup butter**
- **2 cups confectioners' sugar**
- **2 ounces unsweetened chocolate, melted and cooled**
- **1½ teaspoons vanilla extract**
- **3 to 4 tablespoons hot water**
- **Chopped nuts, optional**

1. Let eggs stand at room temperature for 30 minutes. In a bowl, combine the cocoa and water until smooth; cool for 20 minutes. In a large bowl, combine flour, sugar, baking soda and salt. In a bowl, whisk egg yolks, oil and vanilla; add to dry ingredients along with the cocoa mixture. Beat until well blended. In another large bowl and with clean beaters, beat egg whites and cream of tartar on high speed until stiff peaks form. Gradually fold into egg yolk mixture.

2. Gently spoon the batter into an ungreased 10-in. tube pan. Cut through the batter with a knife to remove air pockets. Bake on lowest rack at 325° for 60-65 minutes or until top springs back when lightly touched. Immediately invert pan; cool completely. Run a knife around sides and center tube of pan. Invert cake onto a serving plate.

3. For icing, melt butter in a saucepan. Remove from heat; stir in confectioners' sugar, chocolate, vanilla and water. Drizzle over the cake. Sprinkle with nuts if desired.

CHOCOLATE
CHIFFON CAKE

HOW TO MAKE A CHIFFON CAKE

- Gently fold in the ingredients: Using a rubber spatula, slowly cut down through the ingredients/batter, pull across the bottom of the bowl and bring up part of the mixture.

- To avoid large air pockets in the baked cake, cut through the batter with a knife to break air bubbles.

- Chiffon cakes are done when the top springs back when touched, and the cracks at the top of the cake look and feel dry.

- Cool chiffon cake upside down in the pan. Otherwise, it will collapse and flatten. If your tube pan has legs, invert it onto its legs until the cake is completely cool. If your tube plan does not have legs, place the pan over a funnel or the neck of a narrow bottle until cake is completely cool.

BUTTERY COCONUT BARS

My coconut bars are an American version of a Filipino coconut cake called *bibingka*. These are a crispier, sweeter take on the Christmas tradition I grew up liking.
—**DENISE NYLAND** PANAMA CITY, FL

PREP: 20 MIN. + COOLING
BAKE: 40 MIN. + COOLING
MAKES: 3 DOZEN

- 2 **cups all-purpose flour**
- 1 **cup packed brown sugar**
- ½ **teaspoon salt**
- 1 **cup butter, melted**

FILLING

- 3 **large eggs**
- 1 **can (14 ounces) sweetened condensed milk**
- ½ **cup all-purpose flour**
- ¼ **cup packed brown sugar**
- ¼ **cup butter, melted**
- 3 **teaspoons vanilla extract**
- ½ **teaspoon salt**
- 4 **cups flaked coconut, divided**

1. Preheat oven to 350°. Line a 13x9-in. baking pan with parchment paper, letting ends extend up sides.

2. In a large bowl, mix flour, brown sugar and salt; stir in 1 cup melted butter. Press onto the bottom of prepared pan. Bake 12-15 minutes or until light brown. Cool 10 minutes on a wire rack. Reduce oven setting to 325°.

3. In a bowl, whisk the first seven filling ingredients until blended; stir in 3 cups coconut. Pour over crust; sprinkle with remaining coconut. Bake 25-30 minutes or until light golden brown. Cool in pan on a wire rack. Lifting with parchment paper, remove from pan. Cut into bars.

BUTTERY COCONUT BARS

CINNAMON-APPLE BROWN BETTY

SLOW COOKER

CINNAMON-APPLE BROWN BETTY

If I had to define the "Betty" of Apple Brown Betty, she'd be a smart and thrifty Southern gal with a knack for creating soul-comforting desserts. In this sweet dish, spiced apples are slow-cooked between layers of cinnamon-raisin bread cubes for a wonderful twist on the traditional oven-baked classic.
—**HEATHER DEMERITTE** SCOTTSDALE, AZ

PREP: 15 MIN. • **COOK:** 2 HOURS
MAKES: 6 SERVINGS

- 5 **medium tart apples, cubed**
- 2 **tablespoons lemon juice**
- 1 **cup packed brown sugar**
- 1 **teaspoon ground cinnamon**
- ¼ **teaspoon ground nutmeg**
- 6 **cups cubed day-old cinnamon-raisin bread (about 10 slices)**
- 6 **tablespoons butter, melted**
  Sweetened whipped cream, optional

1. In a large bowl, toss apples with lemon juice. In a small bowl, mix brown sugar, cinnamon and nutmeg; add to apple mixture and toss to coat. In a large bowl, drizzle butter over bread cubes; toss to coat.

2. Place 2 cups bread cubes in a greased 3- or 4-qt. slow cooker. Layer with half of the apple mixture and 2 cups bread cubes. Repeat layers. Cook, covered, on low 2-3 hours or until apples are tender. Stir before serving. If desired, top with whipped cream.

★ ★ ★ ★ ★ 5 STAR TIP

In the case of light brown versus dark brown sugar, the choice is yours! But keep in mind that light brown sugar has a more subtle, delicate taste. If you like a more intense molasses flavor in baked goods, use dark brown instead.

GIANT PEANUT BUTTER ICE CREAM SANDWICH

I created this treat for my husband. Because it can be made ahead of time and frozen, it cuts stress for busy hostesses—and really, who doesn't love peanut butter?

—**JOANN BELACK** BRADENTON, FL

PREP: 30 MIN. • **BAKE:** 20 MIN. + FREEZING
MAKES: 12 SERVINGS

- 2 packages (16 ounces each) ready-to-bake refrigerated chocolate peanut butter cookie dough
- 6 whole chocolate graham crackers, crushed
- 1 cup cold milk
- 1 cup heavy whipping cream
- 1 package (3.4 ounces) instant vanilla pudding mix
- 1 package (8 ounces) cream cheese, softened
- 1⅓ cups creamy peanut butter
- 3 cups vanilla ice cream, softened
- ¼ cup Nutella

1. Preheat oven to 350°. Let dough stand at room temperature 5-10 minutes to soften. Press into two ungreased 9-in. springform pans; sprinkle with graham cracker crumbs. Bake 20-25 minutes or until set. Cool completely.

2. In a large bowl, whisk milk, cream and pudding mix 2 minutes. Let stand 2 minutes or until soft-set. In another large bowl, beat cream cheese and peanut butter until smooth. Add pudding and ice cream; beat until smooth.

3. Spread over one cookie crust. Remove sides of second pan; place crust, crumb side down, over filling. Wrap in plastic wrap; freeze on a baking sheet 4 hours or until firm.

4. Remove from freezer 15 minutes before serving. Place Nutella in a small microwave-safe bowl; cover and microwave at 50% power 1-2 minutes or until smooth, stirring twice. Remove sides of pan; cut dessert into slices. Drizzle with Nutella.

PEACH MELBA TRIFLE

PEACH MELBA TRIFLE

This dream of a dessert tastes extra good on a busy day because you can make it ahead of time. If you don't have fresh peaches handy, use the canned ones.

—**CHRISTINA MOORE** CASAR, NC

PREP: 20 MIN. + CHILLING
MAKES: 12 SERVINGS

- 2 packages (12 ounces each) frozen unsweetened raspberries, thawed
- 1 tablespoon cornstarch
- 1½ cups (12 ounces) fat-free peach yogurt
- ⅛ teaspoon almond extract
- 1 carton (8 ounces) frozen reduced-fat whipped topping, thawed
- 2 prepared angel food cakes (8 to 10 ounces each), cut into 1-inch cubes (about 8 cups)
- 4 small peaches, peeled and sliced (about 2 cups)

1. In a large saucepan, mix raspberries and cornstarch until blended. Bring to a boil; cook and stir 1-2 minutes or until thickened. Strain the seeds; cover and refrigerate.

2. In a large bowl, mix yogurt and extract; fold in whipped topping. In a 4-qt. bowl, layer half of the cake cubes, yogurt mixture and peaches. Repeat layers. Refrigerate trifle, covered, at least 3 hours before serving. Serve with raspberry sauce.

GIANT PEANUT BUTTER ICE CREAM SANDWICH

FUDGE-TOPPED BROWNIES

FUDGE-TOPPED BROWNIES

Why have only brownies or fudge when you can have them both! These exquisite brownies are the ultimate chocolate dessert.
—**JUDY OLSON** WHITECOURT, AB

PREP: 25 MIN. • **BAKE:** 25 MIN. + FREEZING
MAKES: ABOUT 10 DOZEN

- 1 cup butter
- 4 ounces unsweetened chocolate, chopped
- 2 cups sugar
- 2 teaspoons vanilla extract
- 4 large eggs
- 1½ cups all-purpose flour
- 1 teaspoon baking powder
- ½ teaspoon salt
- 1 cup chopped walnuts

TOPPING
- 4½ cups sugar
- 1 can (12 ounces) evaporated milk
- ½ cup butter, cubed
- 1 package (12 ounces) semisweet chocolate chips
- 1 package (11½ ounces) milk chocolate chips
- 1 jar (7 ounces) marshmallow creme
- 2 teaspoons vanilla extract
- 2 cups chopped walnuts

1. In a heavy saucepan or microwave, melt butter and chocolate; stir until smooth. Remove from the heat; blend in sugar and vanilla. Add eggs; mix well. Combine flour, baking powder and salt; add to chocolate mixture. Stir in walnuts. Pour into a greased 13x9-in. baking pan. Bake at 350° for 25-30 minutes or until the top springs back when lightly touched. Cool on a wire rack while preparing topping.

2. Combine the sugar, milk and butter in a large heavy saucepan; bring to a boil over medium heat. Reduce the heat; simmer, uncovered, for 5 minutes, stirring constantly. Remove from heat. Stir in the chocolate chips, marshmallow creme and vanilla until smooth. Add walnuts. Spread over warm brownies. Freeze for 3 hours or until firm. Cut into 1-in. squares. Store in the refrigerator.

WHOLE WHEAT STRAWBERRY SHORTCAKES

WHOLE WHEAT STRAWBERRY SHORTCAKES

Nothing says spring better than a fresh strawberry shortcake. It's heavenly. My mother and I usually make this with strawberries we picked ourselves.
—**SARAH HATTER** BRODHEAD, WI

PREP: 45 MIN. + CHILLING
BAKE: 15 MIN. + COOLING
MAKES: 6 SERVINGS

- 2½ **cups fresh strawberries, hulled, divided**
- 1 **to 2 tablespoons maple syrup**
SHORTCAKES
- 2 **cups whole wheat flour**
- 2½ **teaspoons baking powder**
- ½ **teaspoon salt**
- ¼ **teaspoon baking soda**
- ½ **cup cold butter, cubed**
- 1 **large egg**
- ½ **cup 2% milk**
- ¼ **cup honey**
    Whipped cream

1. In a bowl, thoroughly mash ¾ cup strawberries; stir in syrup. Cut remaining strawberries into ¼-in. slices; add to crushed strawberries and toss to coat. Refrigerate, covered, 1 hour.
2. Meanwhile, preheat oven to 400°. In a large bowl, whisk flour, baking powder, salt and baking soda. Cut in butter until mixture resembles coarse crumbs. In a small bowl, whisk egg, milk and honey until blended; stir into flour mixture just until moistened.
3. Turn onto a lightly floured surface; knead gently 8-10 times. Pat or roll dough to ¾-in. thickness; cut with a floured 2½-in. biscuit cutter. Place 2 in. apart on parchment paper-lined baking sheets. Bake 12-15 minutes or until light brown. Remove to wire racks to cool slightly.
4. To serve, split shortcakes in half. Fill with strawberry mixture and whipped cream. Top with additional whipped cream.

LOVELY LEMON CHEESECAKE

LOVELY LEMON CHEESECAKE

Watch for the oohs and aahs when you present this luxurious cheesecake. The lemon flavor gives it a bright and tangy flair.
—**MARGARET ALLEN** ABINGDON, VA

PREP: 25 MIN. • **BAKE:** 70 MIN. + CHILLING
MAKES: 14 SERVINGS

- ¾ **cup graham cracker crumbs**
- 2 **tablespoons sugar**
- 3 **teaspoons ground cinnamon**
- 2 **tablespoons butter, melted**
FILLING
- 5 **packages (8 ounces each) cream cheese, softened**
- 1⅔ **cups sugar**
- ⅛ **teaspoon salt**
- ¼ **cup lemon juice**
- 1½ **teaspoons vanilla extract**
- 5 **large eggs, lightly beaten**
    Thin lemon slices, optional

1. Preheat oven to 325°. Place a greased 10-in. springform pan on a double thickness of heavy-duty foil (about 18 in. square). Wrap foil securely around pan.
2. In a small bowl, mix cracker crumbs, sugar and cinnamon; stir in butter. Press onto bottom of prepared pan; refrigerate while preparing filling.
3. In a large bowl, beat cream cheese, sugar and salt until smooth. Beat in lemon juice and vanilla. Add eggs; beat on low speed just until blended. Pour over crust. Place springform pan in a larger baking pan; add 1 in. of hot water to the larger pan.
4. Bake 70-80 minutes or until the center is just set and the top appears dull. Remove springform pan from water bath. Cool the cheesecake on a wire rack 10 minutes. Loosen sides from pan with a knife; remove foil. Cool 1 hour longer. Refrigerate overnight, covering when completely cooled.
5. Remove rim from pan. If desired, top cheesecake with lemon slices.

BLUEBERRY-BLACKBERRY RUSTIC TART

My dad would always stop the car on the side of the road in Maine and say, "I smell blueberries!" He had a pail ready to go. Then Mom would bake the wild berries in a cornmeal crust.

—PRISCILLA GILBERT
INDIAN HARBOUR BEACH, FL

PREP: 20 MIN. + CHILLING • **BAKE:** 55 MIN.
MAKES: 8 SERVINGS

- 2 **cups all-purpose flour**
- ⅓ **cup sugar**
- ¼ **cup yellow cornmeal**
- ⅔ **cup cold butter, cubed**
- ½ **cup buttermilk**

FILLING

- 4 **cups fresh blueberries**
- 2 **cups fresh blackberries**
- ⅔ **cup sugar**
- ⅓ **cup all-purpose flour**
- 2 **tablespoons lemon juice**
- 1 **large egg, beaten**
- 2 **tablespoons turbinado (washed raw) sugar or coarse sugar**
  Whipped cream, optional

1. In a large bowl, mix flour, sugar and cornmeal; cut in butter until crumbly. Gradually add buttermilk, tossing with a fork until dough holds together when pressed. Shape dough into a disk; wrap in plastic wrap. Refrigerate 30 minutes or overnight.

2. Preheat oven to 375°. On a lightly floured surface, roll dough into a 14-in. circle. Transfer to a parchment paper-lined baking sheet.

3. In a bowl, combine berries, sugar, flour and lemon juice; spoon over pastry to within 2 in. of edges. Fold pastry edge over filling, leaving center uncovered. Brush folded pastry with beaten egg; sprinkle with turbinado sugar.

4. Bake 55-60 minutes or until the crust is golden brown and filling is bubbly. Using parchment paper, slide tart onto a wire rack to cool. If desired, serve with whipped cream.

LEMON CURD-FILLED ANGEL FOOD CAKE

HOW TO FILL A CAKE

- Insert toothpicks an inch from the top of the cake on all sides as a guide for your knife. Slice the top off the cake with a serrated knife.

- Cut the outline of the tunnel with a small paring knife, leaving a 1-in. shell on each side. Use your fingers to pull out the cake. (Better go ahead and sample it, too!)

- Fill the hollow with lemon or other flavored filling. Replace the top of the cake, then finish with your favorite glaze or other topping.

LEMON CURD-FILLED ANGEL FOOD CAKE

For a sunny angel food cake, I make a filling of mascarpone, heavy whipping cream and lemon curd, and then drizzle the cake with a lemony sweet glaze.

—**LEAH REKAU** MILWAUKEE, WI

PREP: 55 MIN. + CHILLING
BAKE: 45 MIN. + COOLING
MAKES: 16 SERVINGS

- 12 **large egg whites (about 1⅔ cups)**
- 1 **cup cake flour**
- 1½ **cups sugar, divided**
- 1 **vanilla bean (see Note) or**
  1 teaspoon vanilla extract
- ½ **teaspoon cream of tartar**
- ¼ **teaspoon salt**

FILLING
- ½ **cup heavy whipping cream**
- ½ **cup mascarpone cheese**
- 2 **tablespoons confectioners' sugar**
- 1 **jar (10 ounces) lemon curd, divided**
- 1 **cup sliced fresh strawberries,**
  patted dry

GLAZE
- 2 **cups confectioners' sugar**
- 1 **teaspoon grated lemon peel**
- 3 **to 4 tablespoons lemon juice**

1. Place egg whites in a large bowl; let stand at room temperature 30 minutes.
2. Preheat oven to 325°. In a small bowl, mix flour and ¾ cup sugar until blended.
3. Add the seeds from vanilla bean (or extract if using), cream of tartar and salt to egg whites. Beat on medium speed until soft peaks form. Gradually add remaining ¾ cup sugar, 1 tablespoon at a time, beating on high after each addition until sugar is dissolved. Continue beating until soft glossy peaks form. Gradually fold in the flour mixture, about ½ cup at a time.
4. Gently transfer batter to an ungreased 10-in. tube pan. Cut through batter with a knife to remove air pockets. Bake on the lowest oven rack 45-55 minutes or until top springs back when lightly touched. Immediately invert pan; cool completely in pan, about 1½ hours.
5. Run a knife around sides and center tube of pan. Remove cake to a serving plate. Using a serrated knife, cut a 1-in. slice off top of cake. Hollow out the remaining cake, leaving a 1-in.-thick shell (save removed cake for another use).
6. For the filling, in a small bowl, beat cream until it begins to thicken. Add mascarpone cheese and confectioners' sugar; beat until soft peaks form. Fold in ¼ cup of the lemon curd.
7. Line the bottom of tunnel with strawberries. Spoon mascarpone mixture over berries; top with the remaining lemon curd. Replace cake top; refrigerate, covered, at least 4 hours or overnight.
8. For glaze, in a small bowl, mix the confectioners' sugar, lemon peel and enough juice to reach the desired consistency. Unwrap cake; spread glaze over top, allowing some to drip down sides. Refrigerate until serving.
NOTE *To remove the seeds from a vanilla bean, cut the bean lengthwise in half with a sharp knife and scrape out the dark, pulpy seeds.*

**CHERRY GELATIN
SUPREME**

CHERRY GELATIN SUPREME

When I was growing up, this yummy, easy-to-make dessert was always on the menu at the holidays. Years ago, my aunt gave me the recipe, and now when I make it for my family, I think of her.

—**JANICE RATHGEB** BRIGHTON, IL

PREP: 20 MIN. + CHILLING
MAKES: 12 SERVINGS

- 2 **cups water, divided**
- 1 **package (3 ounces) cherry gelatin**
- 1 **can (21 ounces) cherry pie filling**
- 1 **package (3 ounces) lemon gelatin**
- 3 **ounces cream cheese, softened**
- ⅓ **cup mayonnaise**
- 1 **can (8 ounces) crushed pineapple, undrained**
- 1 **cup miniature marshmallows**
- ½ **cup heavy whipping cream, whipped**
- 2 **tablespoons chopped pecans**

1. In a large saucepan, bring 1 cup water to a boil. Stir in cherry gelatin until dissolved. Stir in the pie filling. Pour into an 11x7-in. dish. Cover and refrigerate for 2 hours or until set.

2. In a small saucepan, bring remaining water to a boil. Stir in lemon gelatin until dissolved. In a small bowl, beat the cream cheese and mayonnaise until smooth. Beat in lemon gelatin and pineapple. Cover and refrigerate for 45 minutes.

3. Fold in marshmallows and whipped cream. Spoon over the cherry layer; sprinkle with pecans. Cover and refrigerate for 2 hours or until set.

⑤INGREDIENTS
FROZEN LIME CAKE

I've got just the thing for block parties, cookouts or any time you need a cool dessert. The crust is a snap, and the ice cream and sherbet layers are so delicious. Everyone loves it!

—**KATHY GILLOGLY** SUN CITY, CA

PREP: 15 MIN. + FREEZING
MAKES: 9 SERVINGS

- 1½ **cups ground almonds**
- ¾ **cup crushed gingersnap cookies (about 15 cookies)**
- ⅓ **cup butter, melted**
- 2 **pints pineapple-coconut or vanilla ice cream, softened**
- 2 **pints lime sherbet, softened**
  Whipped topping, optional

1. In a small bowl, combine almonds, cookies and butter. Press onto bottom of a 9-in. square pan. Freeze 15 minutes.

2. Spread ice cream over crust. Cover and freeze at least 30 minutes. Top with sherbet. Cover and freeze 4 hours or overnight.

3. Remove from the freezer 10 minutes before serving. Garnish servings with whipped topping if desired.

GRITS PIE

Simple, Southern and scrumptious, this pie will be a definite hit, even with people who normally don't eat grits. It has the perfect custardy texture.

—**VICTORIA HUDSON** PICKENS, SC

PREP: 15 MIN. • **BAKE:** 30 MIN.
MAKES: 10 SERVINGS

- ¾ **cup water**
- ⅛ **teaspoon salt**
- ¼ **cup quick-cooking grits**
- ½ **cup butter, cubed**
- ¾ **cup sugar**
- 2 **tablespoons all-purpose flour**
- 3 **large eggs**
- ¼ **cup buttermilk**
- 1 **teaspoon vanilla extract**
  Pastry for single-crust pie (9 inches)
  Whipped cream, orange slices or sliced fresh strawberries, optional

1. In a small saucepan, bring water and salt to a boil. Slowly stir in grits. Reduce heat; cook and stir for 4-5 minutes or until thickened. Add butter; stir until melted. Remove from the heat; cool to room temperature.

2. In a small bowl, whisk sugar, flour, eggs, buttermilk and vanilla. Slowly stir into grits. Roll out pastry to fit a 9-in. pie plate. Transfer pastry to pie plate. Trim pastry to ½ in. beyond edge of plate; flute edges. Add filling.

3. Bake at 325° for 30-35 minutes or just until set. Serve warm or cool to room temperature. Garnish with whipped cream, orange slices or strawberries if desired.

BIRTHDAY CAKE FREEZER POPS

On my quest to find birthday cake ice cream —my favorite flavor—I came up with these easy ice pops. Now, instead of going to the store whenever a craving hits, I just head to my freezer.
—**DAWN LOPEZ** WESTERLY, RI

PREP: 20 MIN. + FREEZING
MAKES: 1½ DOZEN

- ⅔ **cup sprinkles, divided**
- 18 **paper or plastic cups (3 ounces each) and wooden pop sticks**
- 2 **cups cold 2% milk**
- 1 **package (3.4 ounces) instant vanilla pudding mix**
- 1 **carton (8 ounces) frozen whipped topping, thawed**
- 2 **cups crushed vanilla wafers (about 60 wafers)**

1. Spoon 1 teaspoon sprinkles into each cup. In a bowl, whisk milk and pudding mix 2 minutes. Let stand 2 minutes or until soft-set. Stir in whipped topping, crushed wafers and remaining sprinkles.

2. Cut a 1-in. hole in the tip of a pastry bag or in a corner of a food-safe plastic bag. Transfer mixture to bag. Pipe into prepared cups. Top with foil and insert sticks through foil. Freeze until firm, about 4 hours. Let stand at room temperature 5 minutes before gently removing pops.

FREEZE IT

MINI PEANUT BUTTER SANDWICH COOKIES

Peanut butter lovers go nuts for these rich little sandwich cookies. To cool down on a hot day, sandwich ice cream between the cookies instead of frosting.
—**KERI WOLFE** NAPPANEE, IN

PREP: 25 MIN.
BAKE: 15 MIN./BATCH + COOLING
MAKES: ABOUT 3½ DOZEN

- 1 **cup shortening**
- 1 **cup creamy peanut butter**
- 1 **cup sugar**
- 1 **cup packed brown sugar**
- 3 **large eggs**
- 1 **teaspoon vanilla extract**
- 3½ **cups all-purpose flour**
- 2 **teaspoons baking soda**
- ½ **teaspoon salt**

FILLING
- ¾ **cup creamy peanut butter**
- ½ **cup 2% milk**
- 1½ **teaspoons vanilla extract**
- 4 **cups confectioners' sugar**

1. Preheat oven to 350°. In a large bowl, cream shortening, peanut butter and sugars until blended. Beat in eggs and vanilla. In another bowl, whisk flour, baking soda and salt; gradually beat into creamed mixture.

2. Shape dough into 1-in. balls; place 2 in. apart on ungreased baking sheets. Bake 11-13 minutes or until set. Remove from pans to wire racks to cool completely.

3. In a small bowl, beat peanut butter, milk and vanilla until blended. Beat in the confectioners' sugar until smooth. Spread filling on bottoms of half of the cookies; cover with remaining cookies.

FREEZE OPTION *Freeze unfilled cookies in freezer containers. To use, thaw cookies and fill as directed.*

NOTE *Reduced-fat peanut butter is not recommended for this recipe.*

TOFFEE-PEAR CRISP BREAD PUDDING

My son loves pear crisp, but one night I was making bread pudding and he asked if I could make both. I compromised by combining two desserts into this one dish. It's fantastic!
—**KURT WAIT** REDWOOD CITY, CA

PREP: 20 MIN. + STANDING
BAKE: 40 MIN. + COOLING
MAKES: 12 SERVINGS

- 1¾ cups 2% milk
- 1 cup butterscotch-caramel ice cream topping
- ¼ cup butter, cubed
- 1 teaspoon ground cinnamon
- ½ teaspoon ground ginger
- 2 large eggs
- 4 cups cubed day-old French bread
- 2 cups sliced peeled fresh pears (about 2 medium)

TOPPING

- ½ cup all-purpose flour
- ½ cup packed brown sugar
- ⅓ cup cold butter
- ⅓ cup English toffee bits

1. Preheat oven to 350°. In a small saucepan, combine milk, caramel topping, butter, cinnamon and ginger. Cook and stir over medium-low heat until butter is melted. Remove from heat.

2. Whisk the eggs in a large bowl; gradually whisk in a third of the milk mixture. Stir in the remaining milk mixture. Add bread; stir to coat. Let stand 10 minutes. Gently stir in pears; transfer to a greased 11x7-in. baking dish. Bake, uncovered, 20 minutes.

3. Meanwhile, for topping, in a small bowl, combine flour and brown sugar; cut in butter until crumbly. Stir in the toffee bits; sprinkle over bread pudding. Bake, uncovered, 20-25 minutes longer or until puffed, golden and a knife inserted near the center comes out clean. Let stand 10 minutes before serving. Serve warm. Refrigerate leftovers.

TOFFEE-PEAR CRISP BREAD PUDDING

CHOCOLATE MEXICAN WEDGING CAKES

CHOCOLATE MEXICAN WEDDING CAKES

Cinnamon adds warmth to this twist on a traditional Mexican treat. Sometimes I add mini chocolate chips to the dough and, after baking, dip the cooled cookies in melted almond bark.

—**JOANNE VALKEMA** FREEPORT, IL

PREP: 20 MIN. • **BAKE:** 15 MIN./BATCH
MAKES: ABOUT 3½ DOZEN

- 1 **cup butter, softened**
- 1¾ **cups confectioners' sugar, divided**
- 1 **teaspoon vanilla extract**
- 1½ **cups all-purpose flour**
- ¼ **cup cornstarch**
- ¼ **cup baking cocoa**
- ½ **teaspoon salt**
- 1¼ **cups finely chopped pecans or almonds**
- ½ **teaspoon ground cinnamon**

1. Preheat oven to 325°. In a large bowl, cream butter and 1 cup confectioners' sugar until light and fluffy. Beat in vanilla. Combine flour, cornstarch, cocoa and salt; gradually add to creamed mixture and mix well. Stir in nuts.
2. Shape tablespoonfuls of dough into 1-in. balls. Place 2 in. apart on ungreased baking sheets. Bake 12-14 minutes or until set.
3. In a small bowl, combine cinnamon and remaining confectioners' sugar. Roll warm cookies in sugar mixture; cool on wire racks. Store in an airtight container.

ICE CREAM COOKIE DESSERT

Our family loves dessert, and this chocolaty, layered treat is one of Mom's most-requested recipes. It's so easy to prepare.

—**KIMBERLY LAABS** HARTFORD, WI

PREP: 15 MIN. + FREEZING
MAKES: 12 SERVINGS

- 1 **package (15½ ounces) Oreo cookies, crushed, divided**
- ¼ **cup butter, melted**
- ½ **gallon vanilla ice cream, softened**
- 1 **jar (16 ounces) hot fudge ice cream topping, warmed**
- 1 **carton (8 ounces) frozen whipped topping, thawed**

1. In a large bowl, combine 3¾ cups cookie crumbs and butter. Press into a greased 13x9-in. dish. Spread with ice cream; cover and freeze until set.
2. Drizzle fudge topping over ice cream; cover and freeze until set. Spread with whipped topping; sprinkle with the remaining cookie crumbs. Cover and freeze 2 hours or until firm. Remove from the freezer 10 minutes before serving.

EASY GRASSHOPPER ICE CREAM PIE

This quick pie is such an ego booster! My family compliments me the entire time they're eating it. A big hit at work potlucks, the pie is good to the last crumb.

—**KIM MURPHY** ALBIA, IA

PREP: 15 MIN. + FREEZING
MAKES: 8 SERVINGS

- 4 **cups mint chocolate chip ice cream, softened**
- 1 **chocolate crumb crust (8 inches)**
- 5 **Oreo cookies, chopped**
- ⅓ **cup chocolate-covered peppermint candies**
  Chocolate hard-shell ice cream topping

Spread ice cream into crust. Sprinkle with cookies and candies; drizzle with the ice cream topping. Freeze until firm. Remove from the freezer 15 minutes before serving.

NOTE *This recipe was tested with Junior Mints chocolate-covered peppermint candies.*

ICE CREAM COOKIE DESSERT

S'MORES CANDY

SALTED PECAN SHORTBREAD SQUARES

My shortbread squares are the ultimate go-to for cookie trays and gift-giving. The buttery caramel and toasted nuts make it tricky to eat just one.
—DIANA ASHCRAFT MONMOUTH, OR

PREP: 25 MIN. • **BAKE:** 25 MIN. + COOLING
MAKES: 4 DOZEN

- 1½ cups all-purpose flour
- 1 cup confectioners' sugar
- ½ cup cornstarch
- 1 teaspoon sea salt
- 1 cup cold unsalted butter, cubed

FILLING
- ¾ cup unsalted butter, cubed
- 1½ cups packed brown sugar
- ½ cup dark corn syrup
- ½ teaspoon sea salt
- ½ cup milk chocolate chips
- ¼ cup heavy whipping cream
- 1 teaspoon vanilla extract
- 4 cups coarsely chopped pecans, toasted

1. Preheat oven to 350°. Line two 13x9-in. baking pans with foil, letting ends extend up sides of pan.
2. Place flour, confectioners' sugar, cornstarch and salt in a food processor; pulse until blended. Add butter; pulse until butter is the size of peas. Divide mixture between prepared pans; press onto bottom of pans. Bake 10-12 minutes or until light brown. Cool on a wire rack.
3. For filling, melt butter in a large saucepan. Stir in brown sugar, corn syrup and salt; bring to a boil. Reduce heat to medium; cook and stir until sugar is completely dissolved, about 3 minutes. Remove from heat; stir in chocolate chips, cream and vanilla until smooth. Stir in pecans. Spread over crusts.
4. Bake 12-15 minutes or until filling is bubbly. Cool completely in pans on wire racks. Using foil, lift the shortbread out of pans. Gently peel off foil; cut into bars. Store in an airtight container.
NOTE *To toast nuts, bake in a shallow pan in a 350° oven for 5-10 minutes or cook in a skillet over low heat until lightly browned, stirring occasionally.*

⑤ INGREDIENTS
S'MORES CANDY

I created my s'mores candy at a time when I couldn't afford store-bought gifts for the holidays. They're awesome for parties and bake sales, and kids love to help.
—STEPHANIE TEWELL ELIZABETH, IL

PREP: 50 MIN. + STANDING • **COOK:** 5 MIN.
MAKES: ABOUT 4 DOZEN

- 2 cups milk chocolate chips
- ½ cup heavy whipping cream
- 1 package (14.4 ounces) whole graham crackers, quartered
- 1 cup marshmallow creme
- 2 cartons (7 ounces each) milk chocolate for dipping
- 4 ounces white candy coating, melted, optional

1. Place chocolate chips in a bowl. In a small saucepan, bring cream just to a boil. Pour over chocolate; stir with a whisk until smooth. Cool to room temperature or until mixture reaches a spreading consistency, about 10 minutes.
2. Spread the chocolate mixture over half of the graham crackers. Spread marshmallow creme over remaining graham crackers; place over chocolate-covered crackers, pressing to adhere.
3. Melt dipping chocolate according to package directions. Dip each s'more halfway into dipping chocolate; allow excess to drip off. Place on waxed paper-lined baking sheets; let stand until dipping chocolate is set.
4. If desired, drizzle tops with melted white candy coating; let stand until set. Store in an airtight container in the refrigerator.

☆ ☆ ☆ ☆ ☆ **READER REVIEW**
"These were a huge hit at a picnic I went to—and far less messy than making them over a fire!"
GINA.KAPFHAMER TASTEOFHOME.COM

PRALINE PUMPKIN TORTE

Perfect for an autumn day, this torte is decadent to the last bite.

—**ESTHER SINN** PRINCETON, IL

PREP: 25 MIN. • **BAKE:** 30 MIN. + COOLING
MAKES: 14 SERVINGS

- ¾ cup packed brown sugar
- ⅓ cup butter
- 3 tablespoons heavy whipping cream
- ¾ cup chopped pecans

CAKE

- 4 large eggs
- 1⅔ cups sugar
- 1 cup canola oil
- 2 cups canned pumpkin
- ¼ teaspoon vanilla extract
- 2 cups all-purpose flour
- 2 teaspoons baking powder
- 2 teaspoons pumpkin pie spice
- 1 teaspoon baking soda
- 1 teaspoon salt

TOPPING

- 1¾ cups heavy whipping cream
- ¼ cup confectioners' sugar
- ¼ teaspoon vanilla extract
  Additional chopped pecans, optional

1. In a heavy saucepan, combine the brown sugar, butter and cream. Cook and stir over low heat until sugar is dissolved. Pour into two well-greased 9-in. round baking pans. Sprinkle with pecans; cool.

2. For cake, in a large bowl, beat the eggs, sugar and oil. Add pumpkin and vanilla. Combine the flour, baking powder, pie spice, baking soda and salt; gradually add to pumpkin mixture just until blended.

3. Carefully spoon batter over the brown sugar mixture. Bake at 350° for 30-35 minutes or until a toothpick inserted near the center comes out clean. Cool for 5 minutes; remove from pans to wire racks to cool completely.

4. For topping, in a small bowl, beat cream until it begins to thicken. Add confectioners' sugar and vanilla; beat until stiff peaks form.

5. Place one cake layer, praline side up, on a serving plate. Spread two-thirds of whipped cream mixture over cake. Top with second cake layer and remaining whipped cream. Sprinkle with additional pecans if desired. Store in refrigerator.

PRALINE PUMPKIN TORTE

GENERAL INDEX

ALPHABETICAL INDEX